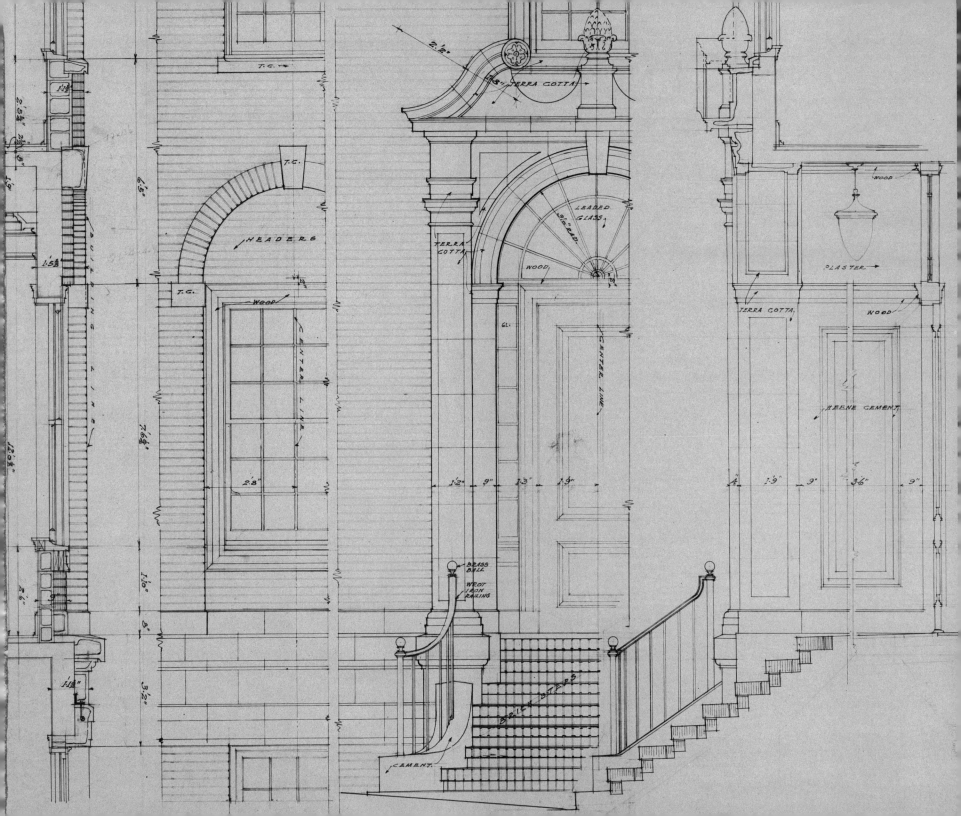

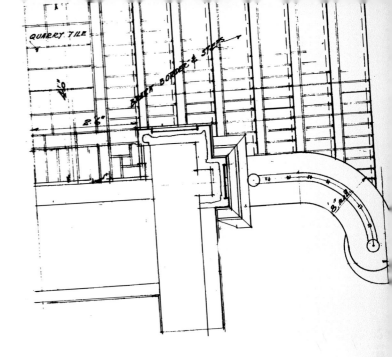

The First 100 Years

Women's University Club of Seattle

1914~2014

Published by Women's University Club of Seattle
First edition, 2013
Printed in China

Design and layout: Kate Basart/Union Pageworks
Project management: Elizabeth Cromwell/Books in Flight
Copyediting: Sherri Schultz
Proofreading: Elizabeth Johnson
Print and color management: iocolor, llp Seattle
Cover images: Women's University Club Archives

ISBN: 978-0-615-82346-1

Women's University Club of Seattle
1105 Sixth Avenue
Seattle, WA 98101-3011
206.623.0402
www.womensuniversityclub.com

Contents

Acknowledgments

These pages tell the story of the extraordinary women who founded, sustained, and led the Women's University Club through a century of change. The Club's leaders have been creative, practical, forward-looking, thrifty, curious, collaborative women, undaunted by challenges. And they remain so today. This book would not be as rich as it is without the constant efforts of the History and Traditions Committee, which maintains the Club archives. It could not have been written without the support of Executive Manager Judy Donnelly and the dedicated efforts of so many members who continue to contribute to this vibrant legacy. We thank each and every one for working to bring this story to you.

Centennial Events Chair: Joy Goodenough

Book Project Director and Editor in Chief: Karen Lane

Editors: Carol Sollie, Sheri Bloch, Maryann Spangler, Julie Moberly

Coordination of Images: Carol Sollie, Sheri Bloch

Writers: Sheri Bloch, Nancy Cleveland, Bonita Dennison, Roseann Hall, Bill Jordan, Diane Kinman, Karen Lane, Bonnie Miller, Judy Ostrow, Barbara Porter, Maryann Spangler

Researchers and Committee Members: Mary Anne Abel, Barbara Beatty, Karen Bonk, Marge Boothe, Marie Cain, Nancy Cleveland, Stevie Crane, Jeanne Crow, Kathie Deviny, Ruth Ellen Elliott, Carol Ellis, Guy Goldsworthy, Judy Gowdy, Roseann Hall, Marilyn Hanson, Gretchen Harrell, Barbara Hering, Katherine Hern, Mary Kraft, Karen Lane, Suzy Lantz, Linda Mattox, Shirley McCarter, Jean McLauchlan, Bonnie Miller, Jane Nelson, Jane Pelly, Lailla Petersen, Philinda Robinson, Carol Sollie, Maryann Spangler, Mimi Stanley, Marcie Stone, Diane Tinker, Judy Waring, Lee Wheeler, Lisa Wood

The Story Begins...

Completion of the Great Northern Railway in 1893 put Seattle on the map. The Alaska gold rush cemented its place as the commercial capital of Puget Sound. With the flood of prospectors eager to strike it rich in the goldfields of Alaska and the Canadian Yukon came men with other ambitions—to run the banks, provide the transport and supply the provisions necessary to send more than 100,000 migrants north.

With them came wives and sweethearts—many of whom were educated in colleges in the Midwest and East. Although outnumbered by men in King County by three to one, adventurous, well-educated single females rode the wave, too.

These women found Seattle to be a wide-open town with unbridled political corruption, lax to nonexistent law enforcement, and little in the way of culture. With ample opportunities for improvement, they quickly joined their predecessors—pioneers of the Washington Territory—in seeking ways to make Seattle a more successful community and a better place to live.

The period from the end of the nineteenth century through the beginning of the twentieth was one of extraordinary civic activism in Seattle, powered by the obvious needs of a young community, increasing wealth in the hands of private citizens, and the spirit of the age. In this environment, visionary, energetic Seattle women spearheaded a variety of civic improvement projects.

In 1896, Libbie Beach Brown played a significant role with her husband in the foundation of Children's Home Society of Washington, an "orphanage without walls." Anna Clise and twenty-three of her friends established Children's Orthopedic Hospital in 1907.

Garden clubs formed, along with parent-teacher associations, ladies' aid societies, and a host of other institutions and committees designed to improve the community and aid the people who lived in it. Their contributions and achievements were celebrated during the 1909 Alaska-Yukon-Pacific Exposition in a designated Woman's Building, now the University of Washington's Cunningham Hall.

In 1910, the Woman's Christian Temperance Union and the Washington Equal Suffrage Association spearheaded the successful effort to gain the vote for women in Washington state. They then launched a recall campaign against Seattle mayor Hiram Gill. Marching under the banner "Ladies: Get Out and Hustle!" they worked with women's clubs throughout the city to oust Gill for breaking his campaign promise to confine brothels to the Pioneer Square area.

Not all energies were directed toward political activism, however. College-educated women in Seattle were also eager to continue learning and expanding their understanding of the world in which they lived. The growing discretionary income of the urban middle class gave them time away from housekeeping, and money to spend on self-improvement as well as social activities.

To this end, the Ladies Musical Club was founded in 1890, the Woman's Century Club was established in 1891 by suffragist Carrie Chapman Catt, and the Woman's Cultural Club was incorporated in 1895. By the second decade of the twentieth century, at least half a dozen clubs were devoted to the social and intellectual needs of Seattle's growing population of literate women.

This is the story of one of them, the Women's University Club.

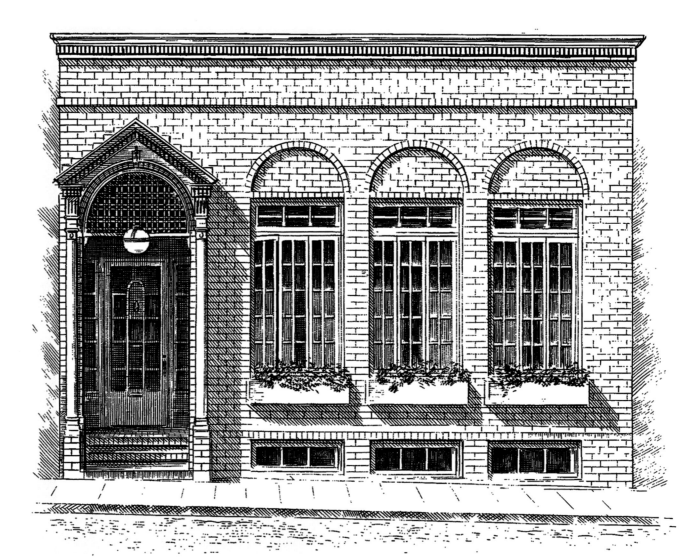

A small one story building at 1250 Fifth Avenue was the first home of the Women's University Club.

Chapter 1

Laying the Foundation ❧

THE WOMEN'S UNIVERSITY CLUB GREW OUT OF THE COMBINED EFFORTS OF fourteen college-educated women with a passion for learning. They wanted a place in downtown Seattle where they could meet to engage in intellectual discussions, experience a unique cultural atmosphere, nurture friendships, and enjoy social activities. The women joined forces to determine the best way to bring their dream to fruition. One hundred years later—and with many achievements to be proud of—the Club celebrates their vision. According to one of the founders, Laura Carr (Mrs. Alvah L.):

"In those early years there were few attractive places in downtown Seattle for women to lunch and dine; automobiles were very scarce, and two-car families were virtually non-existent. Friends in West Seattle and Laurelhurst seemed as far away as if they were in Tacoma. When eastern dignitaries came to town, there was no appropriate place to entertain them, and the college and university women began to feel that they must have a downtown meeting place all their own. The possibility of doing so impressed Mrs. LeRoy [Edith] Backus, who talked about it with her friends and finally called together a group who agreed with her. . . ."

On February 10, 1914, the founders applied in Olympia, Washington, for permission to incorporate as the Women's University Club of Seattle, stipulating that one of the organization's purposes was "to acquire a clubhouse and such other real and personal property as may be desirable." The state of Washington's approval of the Articles of Incorporation was cause for great celebration: the Women's University Club had become a reality. February, the date of application, became the traditional month for the Club's annual Birthday Party.

On February 20, the founders held an organizing meeting in the Henry Building at 1318 Fourth Avenue. They elected interim officers to serve until the annual election, to be held in May: Edith B. Backus, president; Emma C. Nettleton (Mrs. Walter B.), first vice president; Margaret B. Macklem (Mrs. Frank), second vice president; Anna A. Trefethen (Mrs. D. B.), secretary; and Jessie B. Geary (Mrs. H. Logan), treasurer. On February 25, the officers set the initiation fee at $15, yearly dues at $12, and life membership at $150. By the time the first Annual Meeting was held on May 6, again in the Henry Building, 276 women had become charter members.

The board arranged with the Metropolitan Building Company to construct a small one-story building for the Club at 1250 Fifth Avenue, next to the all-male College Club, on land owned by the University of Washington. With the commission of this first building, they laid the groundwork for the next hundred years and beyond.

While the project was still under construction, the board bonded the treasurer for $2,000 and authorized her to sign a contract for a telephone line in time to have the name of the Club in the new phone directory. The board also appointed a

Presidents ❧	
Edith Backus	1914–15
Edith France	1915–16
Florence Heliker	1916–17
Virginia Soliday	1917–18
Anna Trefethen	1918–19
Maria Sumner	1919–20

🐎 In the News

June 28, 1914	Archduke Franz Ferdinand is assassinated: World War I begins
July 4, 1914	Seattle's Smith Tower opens
January 8, 1916	Coliseum Theatre opens in Seattle
July 15, 1916	Boeing Company is founded
April 6, 1917	U.S. enters World War I
May 8, 1917	Lake Washington Ship Canal is completed
November 11, 1918	World War I ends
February 6, 1919	Seattle General Strike begins: 65,000 workers walk off the job for five days
September 13, 1919	President Wilson visits Seattle seeking support for the League of Nations

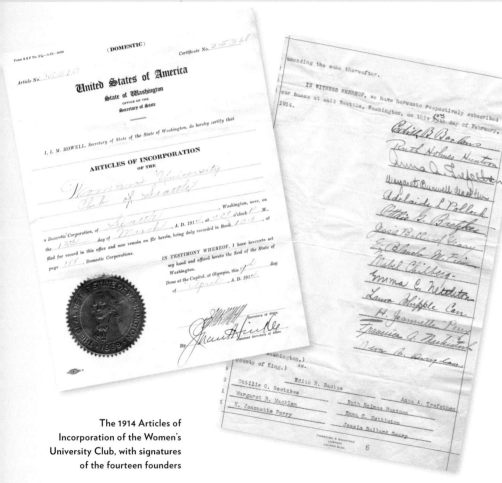

The 1914 Articles of
Incorporation of the Women's
University Club, with signatures
of the fourteen founders

press representative and directed that all publicity connected with the Club was to pass through her hands.

On September 1, the completed building was turned over to the Club. The monthly rental fee, based on a five-year lease, was $150. This small clubhouse would provide members with a comfortable home for the next eight years, though an effort to connect it with the neighboring men's clubhouse was less successful. Laura Carr remembered:

> *The little one-story clubhouse, nestling at the side of the men's big College Club, was not leaning on it for support in spite of facetious remarks. It was entirely from an altruistic standpoint that our Club proposed to have a door constructed in the wall between the two clubs in order that the wives of the College Club members might have the privilege of lunch or tea at the Women's University Club, which project was rejected by the stern males.*

When the trustees took charge of the clubhouse, much work still remained, as Emma Nettleton noted: "The Metropolitan Building Company furnished merely the shell of our home and we had to build our Stately Mansion and even light it!"

By the second Annual Meeting on May 15, 1915, many organizational, management and staffing issues had been resolved. President Backus observed that "the Clubhouse . . . has been found to fill the long-felt need of a downtown meeting place for college women during the day as well as during the evening." She also reported that while the Club's financial condition was solid, austerity was still necessary and she suggested, "To members looking for a return on their investment made by joining this Club, I should like to say: Do not ask, what do I get out of it, but what can I put into it?"

On December 31, 1916, the *Seattle Sunday Times* provided a small glimpse inside the clubhouse: "On Fifth Avenue, in a modest brick building whose interior shows a woman's touch, in rooms most dainty in French gray with old rose hangings, more than 300 women gather, collectively or individually, whenever the spirit moves them, for a social or intellectual time."

The Club's second president, Edith France (Mrs. Clemens J.), thought the clubhouse should become an intellectual and artistic center, with the talents of the members themselves being showcased as much as possible. From the beginning, fueled by the energy and imagination of its members, the Club offered a stunning variety of programs providing the personal enrichment, intellectual challenge, and entertainment envisioned by the founders. The indefatigable Laura Carr gave many superb book reviews, which developed into a Book Review class in 1921; Dr. Mabel Seagrave lectured on medical subjects; and Armene Lamson (Mrs. Otis Floyd) presented a series on world problems. Members with musical talents gave concerts. Students taking French, German, or Spanish classes practiced their fluency—or lack of it—over lunch, while bridge classes and mahjongg brought members to the Club regularly. Classes changed as the interests and needs of members dictated, but the weekly Book Review class, in which a member or guest speaker presents an oral review of a new book, has remained a staple of Club life.

During those early years, many figures of national and international renown also appeared under the auspices of the Club, including progressive journalist Ida Tarbell; Roald Amundsen, leader of the expedition that discovered the South Pole; American poet Vachel Lindsay; and Henrietta Joffre, the wife of Marshal Joseph Joffre of France. For presenters of this caliber, the Club rented space and sold tickets to the public, thus also raising funds for the Club treasury.

Wilma Baker, daughter of George Baker, the gentleman who would become the Club's real estate agent in purchasing the site for the future clubhouse, considered her greatest achievement keeping Ida Tarbell under wraps. Miss Baker was so afraid that someone would steal away the famous muckraking journalist before she spoke to the Club that she almost refused a glimpse of Miss Tarbell to her old friend Laura Carr.

Thanks to the leadership of Mrs. Carr, who was an officer of the Drama League of America, the Club started a drama study group in 1916 that developed into a locally famous performing troupe—the

Edith Backus was a founder and first president of the Women's University Club. Born in New York in 1878, she graduated from Columbia University, married LeRoy M. Backus, and moved to Seattle with him in 1898. Mr. Backus was a real estate developer and, according to Edith's obituary, the son of a "pioneer Seattle family." They had three sons and two daughters. Edith was active in Seattle society and the Garden Club, and played a leading role in founding the Seattle Day Nursery, which provided child care to mothers needing a safe place to leave their young children while they worked outside the home.

Edith B. Backus

Handbag Players. They looked for plays that could be presented using the "handbag technique": each performer carried an article or two of costume in a handbag and then, marching onstage at a signal, turned her back to the audience and donned a hat or wig, eyeglasses or shawl. When she turned to face the audience, she was sufficiently costumed to indicate the character she was playing. The Handbag

GRAND OPENING
OF
WOMAN'S UNIVERSITY CLUB
THEATRE 6th & SPRING

A Million Dollar Spectacle
Only one of its kind in the West

DIRECTOR ARTHUR LUBITCH

OPENING MUSIC, Selection from "The Resurrection," in Chinese

PROGRAM

TOPICS of the DAY International News Reel

The Geezer-Go-Gettum Fillum Company announces the finding of the "Ancient Scroll Expedition" headed by Professoress Amelia Africanus Snodgross of the Sociatatis Mulierum Universitatis.
First Pictures released of the Conversion Rites of Nancy Ann Miller and the Maharajah of Indore Sports.
Drivers race for a five cent purse at Mi-o-my.
Runners from the Olympic Games.

Preview of our Coming Attraction

The Slaughter of the Innocent, starring Dagmar Godowsky & Joseph Saurkrautsky

Educational Film

Behind the scenes in Hollywood during the filming of the "Ninth Heaven" by James Branch Cabell

Feature

"The Lively Bookshop" starring Hollywoods Intelligentsia.

Dance Number

John Gilbert and Mae Murry in person, The Merry Widow Waltz.

Comedy

Mack Sennett's Bathing Beach Band

Finis

A Tragedy in Twenty feet, by the National Board of Censors

All Rights to Critisize Reserved   Patents Pending

Stunt Night playbill promising hilarious entertainment

Players frequently appeared at other clubs and in private homes. During World War I, the money they earned supported the Club's Red Cross work.

Stunt Night, first presented in 1916, was the idea of Willye White (Mrs. Frederic Hall). Club members wrote original skits based on current topics and poked fun at the high and mighty, including themselves, without fear or favor. Years later, the founders either couldn't remember or wouldn't admit who appeared in the first Stunt Night in black long johns and a leopard skin. Members chortled for years over Dr. Seagrave's impersonation of Theodore Roosevelt, as she and Elizabeth Dickerson (playing President Wilson) promised to "clean up the place." Some twenty years later, after numerous performances in the interim, Dr. Seagrave delighted everyone with her caricature of Benito Mussolini.

Sometimes called Jinx Night or Joy Night, Stunt Night was presented more or less regularly for thirty-five years before being discontinued in 1951. Well into the 1980s, when entertainment committees were having their summer meetings to plan the year's programs, a longtime member might be heard to suggest wistfully, "Do you suppose we could revive Stunt Night?"

As the Club grew, securing enough chairs and table settings was a constant struggle. One trustee calculated that each new member required three new chairs. In 1915, the House Chairman lamented that the Club possessed only 70 extra chairs and that it was difficult to see how 200 people attending a Friday afternoon reception could sit down except in relays. The solution lay in an exchange of china and glassware, chairs, and tablecloths with the College Club, which also lacked enough supplies to host a large gathering. In 1916, the second president, Edith France, said with some satisfaction: "Many things we still need, but whatever we have is paid for. We have never lived on future funds. Our bills are paid regularly each month."

Working out an effective governance scheme for the growing Club was a matter of trial and error. In January 1916 two members visited East Coast clubs to learn about effective club policies. Nevertheless, by November the Club had experienced several resignations from the board and from officer positions, a reflection of the amount of time involved—and the other demands on the lives of members—as the Club struggled to define itself and construct a successful organizational and business model.

Progress was made, however. At the 1917 Annual Meeting, secretary Anna Trefethen noted, "I am struck with the increasing solidity and stability of the Club. In its first years, if a vacancy occurred on the Board of Trustees there was an unsettled feeling and the new incumbent went thru quite a period of adjustment before she felt herself to be one of us. The duties of the various officers and chairmen of committees have gradually become so well defined that our ship sails smoothly along in spite of changes in the crew."

Staying true to the founders' intent also demanded vigilance from the Club's leaders. Several charter members, such as Armene Lamson, were ardent feminists, but not all shared their views. At the board meeting in September 1916, Mabel Chilberg announced that Agnes Campbell and Julia Hurlbut were in the city organizing a chapter of the National Woman's Party—which supported women's rights, especially at the ballot box—and would be glad to speak to the Club. Since Campbell and Hurlbut had a political agenda, the board decided that it would be contrary to the Club's mission to invite them—an early example of the careful way the board distinguished the Club as an educational, not political, organization.

Regardless of its early difficulties, the Club was clearly a roaring success. By 1916, although the clubhouse was just two years old, it already seemed too small. Edith Backus proposed, and the board approved, setting aside $5 from each initiation fee in a separate savings account for a larger clubhouse or other development of Club life. To increase the space available, the board appointed a committee to consider adding a second story to the clubhouse, and agreed both

The governing structure of the Club depends on a working board of between five and twenty-one members, each of whom has a defined set of responsibilities—publicity, special lectures and events, or finance, for instance. While the number and duties of trustees change from time to time, the nature of a trustee's work has never varied. Supported by whatever operating committees are deemed necessary, each trustee is completely responsible for every aspect—financial, administrative, and programmatic—of the activities entrusted to her care.

To encourage involvement of as many members as possible and to avoid burnout, trustees are chosen for a single two-year term. The president, who is the presiding officer of the board, is chosen from among former trustees and may serve only a single one-year term. This system has kept the Club relevant and constantly refreshed by the ideas and enthusiasm of new leaders.

to build an additional storage room in the basement for the Club's needs and to rent out the remainder of the space. By summer the Club had a tenant, Mr. Iwao Nichi, manager of the Japan Central Tea Association.

The absence of a library was an early concern, and one was established in 1917. Over time it became known as the Permanent Library, then the Wellesley Room Library, and finally the Wellesley Library. It offered a quiet oasis in the heart of a thriving Club and a busy city. Bookcases were provided by the Club and were initially filled by collecting one book from each member. Members also donated subscriptions to magazines such as *Harper's Monthly* and *Literary Digest*.

The annals of World War I contain only sketchy information about the day-to-day lives of the American women who volunteered to serve in the "war to end all wars" and the contributions they made. But in the Club's archives are letters from members who volunteered for duty overseas and wrote about their experiences. Twelve members courageously embarked on a mission to Europe to bring aid and comfort to American troops and to help civilians in an area ravaged by three years of war.

Mildred Dyer wrote that the first leg of her journey began with an arduous rail trip to New York. To cross the Atlantic, volunteers departed in old passenger ships that transported regiments of soldiers as well as nurses and Red Cross workers. Despite the poor food and living conditions in both England and France, their letters convey a sense of mission and a cheerful disposition while executing their assignments.

Volunteers from the Club traveled to ten different locations in France. Lulie Nettleton worked in the French Alps, for instance, where "about 1200 soldiers came to us each Saturday afternoon for a week of relaxation with our unit." She led hikes and organized wrestling and boxing matches for the soldiers on leave. Later she was stationed in Belgium, where she led tours to art museums and other points of local interest. "[I]ntroducing American lads to [Flemish Baroque painter] Rubens was an illuminating experience," she wrote.

Other Women's University Club volunteers provided aid and comfort at interior hospitals and debriefed soldiers as they demobilized to verify for the Red Cross the dead and missing from their companies. Dr. Mabel Seagrave and Florence Heliker sailed to France with a Women's Overseas Hospital Unit organized by the National American Woman Suffrage Association. Serving under the French, Dr. Seagrave was put in charge of a hospital for 10,000 refugees, where there were no men and the female staff had to do all the heavy work, even making coffins.

In 1919, the French government awarded Dr. Seagrave the Médaille d'Argent in honor of her extraordinary war work. After the war she returned to the United States to practice medicine.

Florence Heliker, left, and Dr. Mabel Seagrave in their French uniforms. Dr. Seagrave wears a medal of honor presented by the French government for her outstanding service.

Excerpts from members' handwritten recollections of their World War I service experiences overseas

"I worked with the American Red Cross in the Home Communication Service in Camp Pontinezen near Brest, France . . . in the spring of 1920. My duty was to interview men before they embarked for the U.S. in an effort to get information regarding their comrades about whom the Red Cross had received inquiries." —*Mabel Chilberg, Red Cross*

"On May 7, 1918 Dr. Mabel Seagrave and I left Seattle for service with the Women's Overseas Hospitals, an organization sponsored by the National Women's Suffrage Organization. At that time our own government did not commission women nurses or physicians so we served under the French government which readily recognized our officers.

"I had trained as an Xray technician, however the Xray machine was lost in crossing the Atlantic and I became an aide in the surgery. . . . We left New York for "destination unknown" and after two weeks arrived in Bordeaux and finally reached our Unit stationed in Labouheyre, France." —*Florence Denny Heliker, French relief hospital*

"All thru the summer of 1918 most of us in Seattle were engrossed in making bandages and knitting socks & sweaters for the overseas, to occupy the tense hours when we knew that our brothers and friends were in deadly peril both on land and sea. . . . I begged the Red Cross to allow me a chance to be useful over there, but the fact that my brother was already in France kept me out. . . . I heard with envy . . . that Florence Dickerson was in Russia with the Y.M.C.A.

"In March of 1919 I was amazed to receive a telephone call from Red Cross: 'Was I still willing to go to France?' Was I? How soon would I be expected to leave? . . . It was a joy to find that Mabel Chilberg and I would be in a small detachment of five girls from the Northwest to relieve workers (in France) who were tired or ill." —*Celia Shelton*

"Having had considerable experience as a mountain climber, I was assigned to Leave Area Work in the French Alps . . . to the position of Out of Doors Recreational Director at San Gervais, just below Chamonois [sic] . . . France. . . . My work overseas . . . exceeded all expectation in interest and real thrills and I hope and believe helped morale in war weary soldiers on leave." —*Emma C. "Lulie" Nettleton, YMCA*

GRACIOUS deed is the delicate
compliment paid to Mrs. Robert
Goodale of Seattle by the Coun-
seil Municipal of Angouleme, which has
made her an hororary citizen of that
place, as follows:

CLUB NEWS AND NOTES

Join the French Class and learn the compliment that has been paid to one of our members in France.

"La Croix rouge americaine qui a secouru avec une touchante generosite les familles francaises eprouvees par le guerre et l'invasion, avait pour deleguee a Angouleme Mme. Goodale.

"Madame Goodale, a accompli sa noble tache avec un devouement et une delicatesse d'ame qui ont touche le coeur de tous ceux qui l'ont vue a l'oeuvre.

"Au moment ou Madame Goodale va quitter Angouleme, le Con-seil Municipal la salue avec respect et pour lui donner un temoignage de reconnaissance, helas! bien faible, il l'a prie d'accepter le titre de citoyenne honraire de la ville d'Angouleme "

The Wednesday Matinee Luncheons, which have become so popular, will have in addition to a special menu each week,

Miss Elizabeth Dickerson, who has been i is now in Archangle. Her friends will be glad to return to Seattle this summer.

Dr. Mabel Seagrave has entire charge of a France. She has an American head nurse wit Mrs. Heliker manages the hospital with the he

Helen Goodale, another member working overseas, was recognized in the *Bulletin* (March 1919).

College Women Hear Reports of War Workers From Overseas

Number of Speakers Discuss Their Experiences From Standpoint of Sisters at Home—Point Out Lessons.

THE luncheon given by the Asso-ciation of Collegiate Alumnae and the College Women's Club, which was held at the Women's Uni-versity Club yesterday, was declared one of the most interesting club af-fairs of the week. The college women of the city approached a subject from a new and interesting angle when they asked the speakers to discuss their experiences overseas from the standpoint of their sisters at home, and to tell what great lesson for womankind throughout the world might be drawn from their observa-tions. Everyone was interested in the first hand reports of the Seattle women who were in overseas service, and as the club has about 200 mem-bers the attendance at the luncheon was very large.

The program, which consisted of a war work symposium, was presented

News report of welcome-home dinner for Women's University Club members and other Seattle women who served overseas during World War I

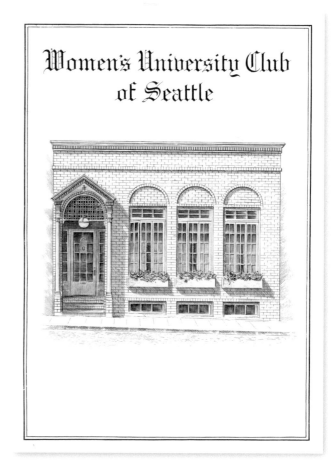

This bookplate was a gift from members Wilma Baker and Edith Backus for the Club Birthday Party in February 1917. A photograph taken by Miss Wills was used to create the image for the printing plate. Every book in the Wellesley Library has had this bookplate inserted inside its front cover for almost a century.

The Library's accession records of purchases and donations date back to 1923. A popular rule was instituted: no time limit on the return of books unless a request had been made for a specific title.

Willye White suggested that the third February Birthday Party become a means of supplying the clubhouse with needed articles. Many beautiful gifts as well as unglamorous household necessities—from furniture to coffee spoons—have been given to the Club as birthday presents. On May 11, 1917, the first Presidents' Reception was held, honoring the outgoing president and her predecessors. So many guests and groups—from sororities to alumnae associations—were coming and going in the clubhouse that Friday afternoon was set aside as a Club Day for members only.

The United States entered World War I on April 6, 1917. The Club purchased a $1,000 liberty bond on June 12, and thrift stamps and war savings certificates were sold to members at the front desk. The board appointed a committee to investigate the most advisable way to accomplish "war work." In short order, the Club set up its own Red Cross auxiliary and let other auxiliaries meet in the clubhouse. Red Cross classes replaced language studies, drama, and writing groups for a time. Members secured donations of linen, rolled bandages, and prepared surgical dressings in an effort to do their part. Club volunteers also adopted a ward in the hospital at Camp Lewis (now Joint Base Lewis-McChord), south of Tacoma, and made many contributions toward the welfare and comfort of the patients, including donating a Victrola and twenty-three new records.

Twelve members of the Club served overseas with the American Red Cross or in other capacities, and many more served on the home front. Members were exempted from paying dues during their service abroad. In January 1918, trustees Mabel Seagrave and Florence Denny Heliker resigned their board positions in order to run a relief hospital in France.

"Since the lessening of Red Cross and war activities, the tearoom will once again be open for afternoon tea. Our famous clam chowder will be served every friday during February."

Bulletin (January 1919)

As the war ended, an especially virulent epidemic of influenza caused an alarming number of deaths worldwide, claiming 1,600 in Seattle alone. Sadly, several of the Club's members succumbed to the pandemic. Since its inception, the Club has paid tribute to deceased members each year through moments for remembrance at its Annual Meeting.

Club life gradually returned to its prewar state. The little clubhouse, however, was bulging at the seams. At the Annual Meeting in May 1919, a Building Committee was appointed to look toward future space requirements, and a "refurnishing tax" of $1 was imposed on each member to help prepare for the furnishing and decorating costs ahead. The members of the Women's University Club eagerly anticipated this next step.

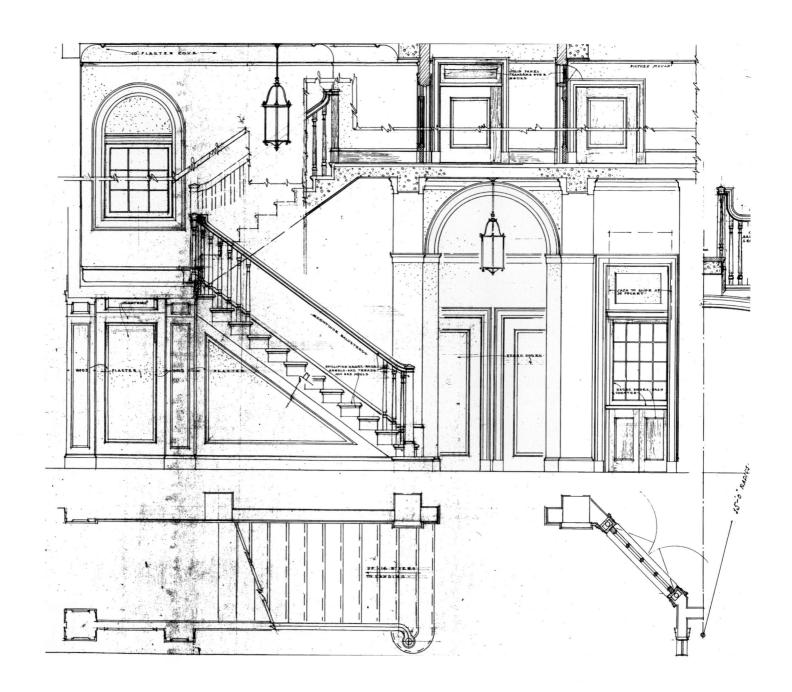

Chapter 2

Building the Structure ❧

AN UNEXPECTED CIRCUMSTANCE PROPELLED BUILDING PLANS FORWARD: the Club faced eviction. In 1920, the Metropolitan Building Company announced plans to erect a hotel (which became the Olympic Hotel) between Fourth and Fifth Avenues, University and Seneca Streets—which meant the clubhouse would be razed along with all the other buildings in that block. The news was disheartening, but members responded with a courageous decision to build their own clubhouse from the ground up. They started a search for the proper location and began the process of rallying members' financial support. In her report on the events of those hectic days, Dr. Mabel Seagrave wrote:

> *Mabel Chilberg, Julia Conway and I met and tried to write some inspiring announcements for a Club dinner to discuss the problem of building a new clubhouse. Mabel Chilberg was to work out the budget, Julia Conway was to put over the bond drive, and I was to wave the flag. The night of the dinner, Mrs. Trefethen presided, and when she introduced me I simply could not get up any enthusiasm so I called on Mabel Chilberg to present the budget. When she got through, everyone was waking up. Mrs. Soliday and Mrs. Bush put forth some very clever verse and I got up my wind. I must have said something, because Mrs. DeSteiguer wrote on a card, 'I will pledge one thousand dollars.' From that moment, I knew we would have a clubhouse.*

The first step was to gain control of Club finances. The board required the Club's various committees to turn their operating funds over to the general treasury, and directed it to pay all bills in the future. The board also proposed, and members approved, an increase in dues. Once these measures were implemented, the Club moved rapidly on two fronts. First, it was necessary to choose a site and design. Second, the project required selling enough bonds to pay for the new clubhouse, as well as securing enough members to support the debt and increased cost of operating a larger building. Two committees were quickly formed—one to supervise construction, one to help fund it.

A membership drive launched on January 14, 1921, challenged each member to secure three new applicants. In addition, the board adopted a policy that permitted members who had been dropped from the roster for nonpayment to be reinstated after six months by submitting a new application and paying the debt they owed the Club. Later that year, the board approved Dr. Seagrave's proposal to raise the initiation fee to $25 effective October 1. The treasurer then directed that $5 from the initiation fee be placed in the Furnishing Fund.

At the Annual Meeting on May 6, 1921, having considered the recommendations of the Building Committee, members approved the following resolution: "That the Club authorize the Board of Trustees to proceed to secure a lot and erect a three-story club building, if on October 1, 1921,

Presidents ❧	
Leda Wilbur	1920–21
Laura Carr	1921–22
Mary Bayley	1922–23
Mary Smith	1923–24
Willye White	1924–25
Alvilde Clark	1925–26
Genevieve Case	1926–27
Blanche Beecher	1927–28
Edna Hadley	1928–29
Lotta Clark	1929–30

August 26, 1920	19th Amendment to the U.S. Constitution gives all American women the vote. Washington women won the vote in 1910
April 24, 1921	Mary Davenport-Engberg becomes conductor of the Seattle Civic Symphony
December 6, 1924	Olympic Hotel opens in Seattle
March 9, 1926	Bertha Landes wins election as Seattle's first woman mayor
May 21, 1927	Charles Lindbergh lands in Paris
October 6, 1927	*The Jazz Singer*, the first talking movie, opens in New York City
July 26, 1928	Boeing Field, Seattle's first municipal airport, is dedicated
October 29, 1929	Stock market crashes

"Many have secured their three new members. With less than ten hours devoted to the actual effort, anyone can get three new members. Have you consulted the lists of college women which are at the Club? Hustle. We want the membership drive over by the end of February. We are going to have the largest and finest college club for women outside of New York, provided YOU do your part."

Bulletin (February 1921)

the resident membership shall have reached 600 or its equivalent, that is $12,000 in annual dues and provided the members shall have subscribed $75,000 in bonds." Through an informal vote, members also expressed their preference for a site south of Pine Street, which was considered the general direction of growth of the downtown business area at that time.

Later in May, the board appointed a committee consisting of Mabel Seagrave, Leda Wilbur (Mrs. Hervey), Willye White, and Anna Trefethen to interview architects Edouard Champney and Abraham Albertson. After their appointment in June, the architects worked throughout the summer of 1921 to prepare preliminary sketches and floor plans.

In a Building Committee report on October 21, Dr. Seagrave requested a brief extension of the deadline to October 31 in order to raise the remaining $2,640 of the required bond subscription. In just a week, by October 29, the goal had been accomplished—$75,000 worth of bonds had been subscribed and a total membership of 600 achieved.

All conditions having been met, the board gave the go-ahead to proceed with the project. The Club made an offer to purchase the corner parcel at Sixth Avenue and Spring Street. One thousand dollars in earnest money was to be applied toward the purchase price of $20,000 ($15,000 in cash and $5,000 in bonds)—with payment of the balance due on January 5, 1922. According to one committee member, the $20,000 purchase price was "considered by real estate men to be a most remarkable bargain."

Members generously pledged to buy bonds "for the purpose of purchasing site and erecting a Club building."

PLEDGE CARD

....1921.

I hereby { increase my subscription to / subscribe for

....Dollars of the bonds to be issued by the Club for the purpose of purchasing site and erecting a Club building.

Signed...

6% Bonds in denominations
$100, $500, $1,000
Ten equal monthly installments, beginning October 1, 1921 and ending July 1, 1922, or payment in full prior to June 1, 1922.

With so many new members, it was not surprising that there might be differing points of view about the purpose of the Club. The board addressed the matter during its November 22, 1921, meeting. President Laura Carr, one of the original incorporators, asked the board to clearly define the character of the Club, stating its objectives and its limitations. The objectives as stated in the Articles of Incorporation were read. The president asked whether "we were at present anything more than a cultural, social Club. Did our Club bring out the finest there was in us?" She pointed out that "our program of activities did not recognize anything that was going on in the world around us," and cited the program of the Women's College Club of Berkeley, California, noting that "it was broader in its scope than our own."

A brief discussion resulted in a proposal to place a complete schedule of activities on the foyer bulletin board and also to print it in the monthly announcements, to better promote Club programs. There was a strong expression in favor of resuming the speaker luncheons and scheduling them as frequently as possible. Laura Carr urged planning new activities at once to help maintain the interest of the large group of new members.

The chairmen responded with vigor. Along with the focus on the new clubhouse, activities increased and opportunities for learning and enjoyment were abundant. The proposed lineup of classes included a new Current Topics Circle, which seemed to be a direct response to Mrs. Carr's request, covering current events around the world, art, music, drama, education, religion, and recent books.

Under the leadership of Dr. Belle Baldwin (Mrs. Albert D.), the 1922 Book Review class featured a review of *His Children's Children*

"A dance was held, the first in a series of three to be given for the benefit of the Building Fund. Season tickets may be bought at the Club for $6.00 (for member and guest). Admission for two at a single dance $2.50."

Bulletin (December 1920)

by Arthur Train, along with *The Hall and the Grange* by Archibald Marshall and *Eminent Victorians* by Lytton Strachey. Drama groups studied *Back to Methuselah* by George Bernard Shaw and heard a reading of Eugene O'Neill's *The Emperor Jones*.

Books could be checked out from the circulating library for a fee of $2 per year, which also entitled the member to join the book review circle of Bess Brehm (Mrs. George). A Music Appreciation series and the Glee Club appealed to music-loving members.

Not all the emphasis was on education. A highlight of members' June social calendars was the annual picnic at Lochkelden, the home of Alice Denny (Mrs. R. H.). A chartered boat left Madison Park at 10:30 A.M., returning at 4:30 P.M.; guests were warned that there were no other boat connections. The program of activities varied. On one occasion, new members waited on tables. Later came a contest of strength and agility between old and new members, causing much hilarity. Tickets were $1 including boat fare, field events, and the luncheon.

A Halloween Cabaret *Bulletin* announcement promised amusing October entertainment: "Ghosts will serve at the 6:30 dinner. A quartet of black cats will sing and sprites and goblins will play spooky pranks on the assembled guests." A hat-trimming contest, with prizes awarded for the most artistic creations, provided a mixture of fun and philanthropy to benefit the Children's Orthopedic Hospital in November 1921.

Swimming groups formed, meeting on Tuesday mornings and Wednesday afternoons at the YWCA pool and requiring a physical exam costing $1. Saturday afternoon ice-skating parties would soon be a popular addition to the exercise agenda.

In January 1922, with the Spring Street lot purchase completed, the survey of property was presented to the board. As it reviewed plans for the new building, the board decided to accept a design that included only one floor of bedrooms, as proposed by the Plans Committee. These rooms were to be rented to women on a short- or long-term basis, with dining privileges and housekeeping included. Members of women's clubs in

Always eagerly anticipated, annual summer picnics were hosted at Club members' homes. In this photograph, members enjoy an afternoon on the shores of Lake Washington (1923).

the president to sign the excavation contract. At a meeting on May 9, 1922, the board agreed to take out a $40,000 loan to pay for construction.

Weekly board meetings emphasized the need for timely decisions as the building took shape. Willye White, chairman of the Furnishing Committee, remembered, "While I was East . . . the plans were completed and sent to me to mark light fixtures and floor plugs, and on the train from Kansas City to Los Angeles, I spent my entire time arranging and re-arranging bits of cardboard, cut by scale to represent furniture, in order to place the lights with some sort of accuracy."

Having instituted a new book of accounts, the board expanded responsibilities of the Finance Committee to include establishing financial policies, preparing budgets for submission to the board, and overseeing the Club's bookkeeping system and staff. No purchases exceeding $5 could be made without Finance Committee approval. Once the new clubhouse was opened, budget-saving measures included purchasing lightbulbs in ten-dozen lots to get an 18 percent discount and issuing clean bath towels to residents every other day, rather than daily, to reduce laundry costs.

other cities would also be able to use their exchange privileges to stay at the Club while visiting Seattle.

The Building Committee requested a meeting with the Club president, Mary Bayley (Mrs. Frank S.), to draw up a list of responsibilities for the chairmen of the Finance, Plans, Ways and Means, Furnishing, and Building Committees. The detailed descriptions of the individual committees' duties won quick approval.

On further reflection, the board decided in March 1922 to have drawings made for an additional floor of bedrooms so that bids could be requested for a four-story building. They also instructed

President Laura Carr's report to the Annual Meeting in May 1922 praised the members who were working to bring the clubhouse to fruition.

> *"Do you know that we are serving a Club Luncheon consisting of an entrée or a salad, hot rolls, and coffee for 35 cents? This is in addition to our regular a la carte menu. Afternoon tea service now 25 cents per person. We wish to be of the greatest possible service to our members and will be glad to receive requests or suggestions at any time."*
>
> Bulletin (March 1922)

> *"I wish I had the power to make you feel the strength there is in the united efforts of hundreds of women, each doing her small share, as it reveals itself to those in a position to see it work out. We made a great impression on the public when we decided to build. . . . A club of women that can sell over $75,000 worth of bonds in the midst of unsettled business conditions and, in the same year raise $1,225.49 for furnishings, besides saving $1,200 out of its membership dues, is my idea of a live, financially sound and well managed organization that deserves the confidence both of its members and of the public and need not fear the future."*

In June the board authorized the chairman of the Furnishing Committee to place an order with Tacoma Cabinet Works for

"Now, that leaves three members not serving on committees."

bedroom furniture. Individuals and groups were solicited to take on the task of supplying accessory furnishings for the various rooms. Bedrooms were fitted by Leda Wilbur and by local alumnae from Smith College, Vassar, Mount Holyoke, Wisconsin, and Michigan. Wellesley members attended to the Library, and trustees (former and present) took responsibility for the Trustees' Room. Donors received recognition with their names on a plaque on the door. Effie Raitt, director of the University of Washington School of Home Economics and also House Trustee, played an essential role in planning the operations of the residential floors. By October, the board was deep into budgeting for the costs of food, laundry, and other services that would be required by residents, whom it referred to as houseguests.

On October 10, 1922, trouble struck. The underground spring for which Spring Street was named caused so much dampness in the basement that the board had to authorize waterproofing on the walls and floor of the Ballroom, an unexpected $600 expense.

Then the Tacoma firm that was to furnish the bedrooms declared bankruptcy, exactly six weeks before the scheduled opening of the Club. Furnishing Committee Chairman Willye White wrote, "We had taken such pride in ordering everything early and working out all the details of color so that there would be no frantic rush or hasty decision. Then, in a minute, to find *nothing* done and only six weeks to do it all over...." The furniture was cut and ready to assemble, but it was locked in a bonded warehouse. After many trips to Tacoma to talk to the bank and bonding company, the Club was granted permission to go elsewhere. But only three weeks remained. The Furnishing Committee arranged with Frederick & Nelson, Seattle's leading department store at the time, to take on the job. Willye White told the members, "They took our original designs and, with only a few minor changes, made and loaned us everything we needed for the opening."

Residents happily moved into their new home in November 1922. According to Mrs. White, the new clubhouse had "the best equipped kitchen in the city, a dining room with 100 chairs and 16 tables . . . 49 attractive bed rooms including one suite . . . a beautiful card room, a restful comfortable library, a drawing room with tremendous possibilities and an auditorium with 450 chairs. . . ." The building cost $115,027.46, not including the lot and excavation.

On December 9, 1922, it was finally time to celebrate the formal opening with a gala event for members only. A moving and dramatic dedicatory ceremony, written by Alvilde Clark (Mrs. Everett), was presented on that memorable date. The script reads in part:

Miss Marianne King

Mrs Florence Denny Heliker

Mrs. W. A. Major

Mrs. John Wilson

Miss Jessie Keith

Mrs Fordyce Gorham

Miss Edith Van Winkle

Mrs. H. H. Denham

Forty-six rag rugs were crafted by members to match different rooms in the new building.

And we greatly rejoice in the consummation of so great a work—yet this structure, desirable in its every aspect, is but the outward symbol of the high aspirations which actuated it, of the lofty ideals which shall perpetuate it. And we dedicate it this Ninth day of the Twelfth month, in the Year of our Lord, the Nineteen Hundred and Twenty-second, to the pursuit of worthier ambitions, to the promotion of a closer fellowship, to the attainment of purer ideals, to [the] accomplishment of nobler purposes and to the realization of a fuller life.

On January 13, 1923, at the first membership meeting in the new building, the president's brief address of congratulations—"to the committees and workers who had achieved such success in the building they now enjoyed, with so much harmony among them"—aroused a swell of enthusiasm. The Club gave three cheers for Dr. Mabel Seagrave, the chairman of the Building Committee, followed by three cheers for President Mary Bayley.

The Club indeed had a beautiful new facility. However, it was also operating a new business, a gentlewoman's residential hotel, as well as making the lecture hall and dining room available for rent. The board and committee chairmen faced a tall order in determining how to manage such an enterprise, meet the needs of members, cover expenses every month, and pay the mortgage and bonded indebtedness. In her last President's Message in May, Mrs. Bayley added a cautionary note: "The Club is built and now we must go forward. Here is the promised land but as yet we may not possess it. First we must earn it. This building that we see and call our own, we do not own."

"The rug makers need more materials.
They need both old and new.
They also need scissors and thimbles.
But most of all they need YOU!"

Bulletin (October 1922)

The Club's decision to provide guest rooms was an immediate success. At the May 1923 Annual Meeting, the Furnishing Committee reported: "From the beginning the Committee had a strong desire to create an air of individuality in the rooms furnished. We sought simplicity and durability and that elusive thing called 'charm.'" According to the *Bulletin* on June 1, 1923, "Twenty-four of the 25 who have been at the Club this year have signed up for next year. Members who wish to live at the Club next year must make reservations by July 1. Rooms with board range from $60 [per month] to $87.50 (with private bath)."

In addition, the September *Bulletin* announced that the clubhouse "had been kept well filled with exchange privilege guests, who have been most laudatory in their praise of our Club facilities. Our register shows 186 guests during July and August. The list contains some well-known names of presidents and deans of colleges, physicians, and other professional women, along with members of twelve of the fourteen exchange college and university clubs."

Over the next several years, the Club sponsored lectures and theatrical performances open to the public. Sometimes, when especially large audiences were expected, the venue was outside the clubhouse. The Stuart Walker Players and Angna Enters, dancer and mime, were presented at the Metropolitan Theatre, and the Denishawn Dancers from Los Angeles, best known today for having trained Martha Graham, appeared at the Masonic Temple (now the Egyptian Theatre). Author-adventurer Richard Halliburton appeared at the clubhouse, as did English novelist Hugh Walpole. Club activities frequently made the news, since local newspapers at that time were eager for society items; Club *Bulletins* often advised members to "watch newspapers for details."

Effie I. Raitt, for whom the University of Washington's Raitt Hall was named, was a woman with an enterprising talent for organization. When she became director of the School of Home Economics in 1912, it consisted of one other instructor and was housed in a leaky shack on the western edge of campus. Determined to obtain a new building for the three-year-old school, Professor Raitt enlisted the aid of the Federated Women's Clubs in the state and lobbied the legislature. Nor was she above a bit of gentle guile. She invited legislators to a luncheon in the shack and, as luck would have it, it was a rainy day. The roof leaked steadily, lunch was soggy, and a few days later the legislature of 1915 appropriated funds for a new structure for home economics. Professor Raitt guided the school until her death in 1945.

From "Raitt Hall," *Liberal Arts Quadrangle,* http://www.washington.edu/home/lib_quad.html (accessed October 7, 2012)

The first Sports Clothes Ball, an annual event sponsored by the Women's University Club with conspicuous success, took place in the Club's own Ballroom in 1924. The dance appeared as a benefit for the new clubhouse, and immediately proved so popular that it became a fixture on the calendar. The *Seattle Sunday Times* reported on May 4, 1924:

> *"The ballroom obligingly turned itself into the most charming of country club settings with brilliantly striped awnings along the windows, gay parasols, wicker chairs and bright colored cushions, and here and there masses of fruit branches. The punch was served under a bower of spring flowers on the stage and the supper in the main dining room upstairs."*

Celebrating its tenth anniversary, the Women's University Club held its annual luncheon at the clubhouse on Saturday, April 5. One of the interesting events, for which this club is becoming famous, is the offering of a prize each year for the best play written by a member. The play selected is produced at the birthday luncheon the following year by a cast of club players.

Seattle Times, April 13, 1924

The Club's literary resources had expanded considerably since the move to a larger building. In 1928, the Book Review class and other members added 71 books to the Library, bringing the total to 847. The Library also had 14 magazines subscriptions, 4 donated by members and the remainder purchased with $25 approved by the board and $14 contributed by residents.

By March 1929, there was no question that the Women's University Club had moved into the twentieth century with its sponsorship of a lecture series entitled Safe Driving. The president of the University of Washington Alumnae Association proposed a partnership with the Club to sponsor two series of five lectures each on the topic. One series would be for teens and one for adults. The board decided that the Club would furnish the auditorium for the lectures, a contribution valued at $157, if the Alumnae Association agreed to pay any additional expenses. Both organizations would sell tickets and divide net profits equally. The Club's profits from the driving school totaled $84.75.

The Women's University Club was the first clubhouse in the city where members could live, attend cultural events, and enjoy social affairs. Pictured are: 1. Edith Backus, founder and first president. 2. Dining room, "which featured richly brocaded orange and gold drapes imported from Paris." 3. Mary Bayley, president. 4. Spacious auditorium/ballroom with supper room and well-equipped theater stage. 5. Entrance to the new building at Sixth Avenue and Spring Street.

THE WOMEN'S UNIVERSITY CLUB *dinner dance Friday, one of the principal events on its calendar for the season, filled the clubhouse with a brilliant gathering of members and their friends. The sketch below, by a Times artist, pictures the guests assembling in the ballroom.*

A *Seattle Times* artist's sketch portrays glamorous guests at a Friday night dinner dance in the new Ballroom.

Linens Committee

At the time the Women's University Club was founded, a woman's sewing basket was never far from her favorite chair. Embroidering household linens, darning socks, replacing buttons, turning cuffs, and dozens of other small domestic sewing chores were the frequent occupation even of women of means.

It was natural for the thrifty founders to put these skills to work in service to their beloved Club. While the new building was under construction in 1922, preparing furnishings for the public rooms and the many new bedrooms moved into high gear under the general direction of the Furnishing Committee. They exhorted members: "Please check the things you can do— don't be too modest—be generous with your time." The list of work was exhausting: hemming, hemstitching, embroidering, making rugs and pillow covers, sewing chair pads and crafting lampshades, appliquéing bedspreads and making curtains. There were 150 tea napkins to be finished with a crocheted picot edge and ten dozen towels to be hemmed and monogrammed.

Once the new building was completed, maintaining the linens fell to a new Linens Committee under the House Trustee. During the 1930s, this committee played an especially important role. With funds so scarce, repurposing worn items saved considerable sums. Old rugs were cut down for smaller spaces; bed linens were turned and turned again; new borders refreshed old blankets. In 1936, committee members made fifty-six napkins from well-worn tablecloths, hemmed eighteen linen table coverings, finished sixty-six powder room towels, and made six pairs of curtains for the private baths.

But it wasn't all work. Committee members found great satisfaction in "these pleasant after-noons of sewing." They were a time for fellowship, and the members were further rewarded by the pleasure their efforts brought to the residents. The 1955 House Trustee recalled that Linens Committee members "always took time to do the little extras . . . for houseguests."

Even in 1960, when a new stage curtain was bought, the committee made the old one into draperies for some of the bedrooms. By the end of that decade, however, there were few women who still sewed and fewer residents. For a brief time, the Linens Committee became the Sewing Committee, and then went out of business with the departure of the last houseguest in 1974.

Chapter 3

Surviving the Depression ❧

THE THIRTIES BROUGHT DAUNTING CHALLENGES. AS THE GREAT DEPRESSION tightened its grip on the country, the Club's membership dwindled—from a peak of 825 in 1927 to fewer than 600 in 1932. Several trustees on the board were forced by economic circumstances to resign, adding a loss of leadership to the loss of membership. As early as September 1929, before the stock market crash, the board was sufficiently alarmed to launch a special membership drive.

These were years of unremitting efforts by the Club's leaders to keep the organization afloat financially while continuing to offer the extraordinary range of programs its members had come to expect. The board created a new membership category, associate member, in 1932, allowing women without full educational requirements to participate in Club activities. Concessions that would have been unthinkable in earlier years were enacted, including waiving entrance fees, deferring dues payments, and—at least for a time—allowing guests of members to participate in individual classes for a fee of 25 cents.

The board laid off staff and slashed salaries, briefly increased the luncheon price by 25 cents, considered raising guest room rates, and even speculated whether, as part of their search for revenue, "the best use of the auditorium would be to make it into a 'little theater' as soon as possible." Despite their efforts, by September 1929 the Club had incurred a deficit of $1,890.33 since the start of the fiscal year and secured a bank loan to pay its bills.

Red Top cabdrivers blackballed the Club in 1930, refusing to pick up or drop off passengers because Club employees were not unionized. When the Teamsters refused to make deliveries, Club members assumed duties such as picking up and delivering food, flowers, and other items. Labor disputes simmered throughout the thirties. In September 1939, after the Supreme Court ruled that employees were not required to unionize unless they wished to, the House Trustee met with representatives of the American Federation of Labor to discuss unionizing Club employees, who eventually decided not to join a union.

In spite of hard times, Club life was undiminished. Classes offered in January 1930 included Modern Art, Early American Furniture, Book Review, International Relations, French and German Conversation, Short Story Writing, Garden Study, The Bible as Literature, and Travel. Book Reviews included *My Early Life* by Winston Churchill, *Years of Grace* by Margaret Ayer Barnes, *The Good Earth* by Pearl Buck, and *The Second Twenty Years at Hull-House* by Jane Addams. Thornton Wilder gave three lectures, including one on *The Bridge of San Luis Rey*. Also at the podium was Nellie Cornish, who founded the Cornish College of the Arts in Seattle the same year the Women's University Club was incorporated. Within three years, Cornish had become the largest music school west of Chicago.

Presidents ❧	
Susan Pease	1930–31
Frances MacBride	1931–32
Lucy Davidson	1932–33
Mary Watts	1933–34
Dorothy Falknor	1934–35
Margaret Lyle	1935–36
Mayme Hemphill	1936–37
Fredericka Shaw	1937–38
Edith Carlson	1938–39
Annette Bocker	1939–40

In the News

December 10, 1930	Denny Regrade is completed
August 13, 1932	Seattle swimmer Helene Madison wins three gold medals at the Olympics in Los Angeles
November 8, 1932	Franklin D. Roosevelt is elected president; Warren Magnuson is elected to the State House
June 23, 1933	Seattle Art Museum opens in Volunteer Park
December 5, 1933	21st Amendment to U.S. Constitution is ratified; Prohibition ends
July 28, 1935	Boeing B-17 prototype makes its maiden flight
May 1936	Margaret Mitchell's *Gone with the Wind* is published
August 14, 1936	University of Washington rowing crew wins a gold medal at the Olympic Games in Berlin
July 7, 1937	Japan invades China; beginning of hostilities in the Far East
July 29, 1938	Ivar Haglund opens a fish and chips stand at Pier 54

"I'm sorry, Madam President, there won't be any treasurer's report this month because we have a deficit."

t the start of the Depression, the board had appointed a Special Finance Committee to help navigate the storm. A lawyer was consulted regarding the amount of dues income required to operate the Club "in a proper sort of way." He concluded that although the proposed dues of $3 per month were inadequate, the Club could not charge more. The board decided to recommend dues of $36 per year at the annual business meeting in May 1930 and also began to stock and sell cigarettes and popular candies.

The board consulted a law firm about whether assessments could be levied on members. The reply: "An assessment may be levied but collection cannot be enforced." Instead, the board sent a notice to Club members in November 1930 reminding them, "The large number of small bills which are outstanding is forcing the Club to borrow money from the bank to meet current bills. If these accounts were promptly paid, this situation would be avoided."

Early in 1931, the board again offered inducements to recruit new members. In January, thirteen new members were proposed; there were forty-three more by March, and another ten in April. Nevertheless, the number of new members was insufficient to stop the steep decline. In May the board approved a resolution allowing members "dropped in 1931–32 for non-payment of dues [to] be eligible for re-election on account of the serious and unequalled economic condition of the present time. . . ." The treasurer further proposed, and the board approved, extending for another six months the deadline for payment of past-due Club bills, providing the member paid at least $1 per month.

Although the board initially sought to balance the budget via cuts in staff, salaries, and general expenses in combination with increases in food and room charges, the strategy became self-defeating as general price levels fell. In November 1932 the Special Finance Committee recommended that the price of rooms be reduced; that the prices of dinners be lowered to 75 cents and 90 cents; that luncheon prices be reduced to 35 cents, 45 cents, and 60 cents; and that the minimum service requirement in the dining room be reduced to 25 cents. The following May, the board decided that expenses of board members would not be reimbursed until the Depression was over, but that $30 per year, the equivalent of two lunches and two dinners per month, would be allowed to the president. On top of everything else, things continued to wear out. When the cost to replace worn china was estimated to be $175, the board found a way to obtain what was needed through trading in old china, and meeting the balance of the purchase price with a lesser sum.

The board initiated yet another membership campaign in August 1933: 100 members would be admitted without any initiation fee, provided they remained in the Club for a period of two years or paid a fee of $25 if they resigned sooner.

Fortunately, the financial condition improved a bit. By November there were so many new members that a special table in the dining room was prepared for them on Club Day, then held each Wednesday, hosted by one member from the board and one from the Hospitality Committee. That year, the Christmas Fund collected a remarkable $222.32, which was dispensed to fifteen employees and the postman.

With money tight and few people at liberty to travel, the Club drew on local resources or out-of-town visitors who were in Seattle for other reasons as a source of speakers and programs. College presidents were always popular speakers. Ellen Fitz Pendleton, president of Wellesley, was a guest of the Club as well as a speaker during her visit to Seattle. Dr. Robert D. Leigh, president of Bennington College, and Dr. Dexter Keezer, president of Reed College, also spoke.

Members organized bimonthly art lectures by well-known Seattle artists and invited Bertha Landes (Mrs. Henry), a member and former Seattle mayor, to give two lectures on the structure of city government and the importance of women in elective office as "civic housekeepers."

Simple pleasures such as card games and dances filled the schedule. Ballroom dancing classes for members, their children, and guests were expanded. The Contract Bridge series took off, with twenty-eight tables reserved for first lessons. Soon the average attendance on Tuesday and Friday nights was ten tables of card players.

Members never tired of hearing about the latest books. At the top of the list in 1931 were Can Europe Keep the Peace? *by Frank H. Simonds;* The Barretts of Wimpole Street, *a play by Rudolf Besier;* Only Yesterday, An Informal History of the 1920s *by Frederick Lewis Allen; and a biography of Jenny Lind, the singer often known as the "Swedish Nightingale."*

Stunt Night, which had been such an important part of the Club's life during World War I, was revived during the thirties. In 1936, Stunt Night featured a "Meeting of the International Women's Conference in Ethiopia." According to the March *Bulletin*, "All members of the Women's University Club are urged by His Majesty, Haile Selassie, to attend in costumes of the various nations" (and advised by the Club to "plan entertainment for husbands and children elsewhere"). The price of admission was 85 cents.

With such an abundance of activities, newspaper reporting of Club events became so ubiquitous that limits had to be imposed. The board approved a resolution stating that "no reporter shall come to any class or lecture at the Club without permission of the head of the Department concerned."

Keeping the dining room full of customers and the clubhouse in good repair was a constant challenge. Numerous committees were in charge of the many details involved in managing the facility: Appointments, Auditorium, Dining Room, Flowers, Linens, Rooms, and Communications. Wednesdays continued to be Club Day during the summer of 1934. The *Bulletin* promised: "The luncheon menu will be particularly attractive that day. Guest cards for the dining room for the summer are available at your request at the office. Your town friends as well as your out-of-town guests will appreciate this courtesy."

Mr. and Mrs. Judson Falknor are receiving congratulations of their friends upon the birth of a son, April 1, at Swedish Hospital. Mrs. Falknor is president of the Women's University Club.

*   *   *

Tap-dancing members entertained at Stunt Night.

Filling the upstairs bedrooms was also an important source of revenue. Members were advised: "Please do not forget that if you know anyone from out of town who will be in Seattle for a few days, she may obtain an attractive room at the Club for $1.35 per day (including breakfast). Room with bath (including breakfast) will be $2.00." In an effort to find permanent residents, the Club sent 340 letters to high school teachers advertising the availability of rooms. The Room Chairman also sent personal letters to the presidents of the Business and Professional Women's Club and the Seattle Grade School Teachers' Club, the principal of the Central School, and the director of the Child Study Laboratory at Seventh and Marion, among others. "To all of these, the privilege was extended of allowing members of their group to live at the Clubhouse."

The Club's first pregnant president, Dorothy Falknor (Mrs. Judson), gave birth in April 1935. She was not present at the board meeting on April 9, but sent a lovely corsage to each board member. She had begun the process of formalizing the Club's long-range planning, appointing a "Forward Looking" Committee chaired by Frances Owen (Mrs. Henry B.). Margaret Lyle (Mrs. Stanley) took over as president a month later.

In spite of vigorous cost-cutting and several successful membership drives, in 1935 the Club was unable to pay its bondholders and maintain sufficient funds for operations. A total of $100,000 in bonds had originally been issued to build the clubhouse, 500 in $100 denominations and 100 in $500 denominations. Bondholders were paid 6 percent interest per year, with the bonds maturing July 1, 1942. The Special Finance Committee negotiated new terms by extending the maturity date to July 1, 1956, and reducing the interest rate to 3 percent per year. The new schedule provided a reserve fund, over and above the amount necessary to operate and maintain the property, to retire at least $1,000 per year of outstanding bonds. The president and secretary were authorized to enter into an agreement with a trust company and the consenting bondholders to effect these modifications.

At the Semiannual Meeting in November, the Special Finance Committee was authorized to send a letter to bondholders informing them of the situation and the proposed plan, and requesting their consent to this change. (It wasn't until 1944 that 100 percent of the bondholders consented to the refinancing program, at which point the Club turned management over to its trustee.)

By 1937, the Club's financial situation was noticeably improving. More than $2,000 in bonds had been retired, leaving $85,500 outstanding. The auditor's report described the Club's finances as satisfactory, and the dining room even made a profit. In a spirit of optimism, pay raises were awarded to the staff.

In May, the title of house manager was changed to Club manager, with an attendant increase in responsibilities. The role of publicity representative was given to a new Publicity Trustee, appointed at the May 24 board meeting under the incoming president, Fredericka Shaw (Mrs. Gordon T.).

Major improvements to the fifteen-year-old clubhouse over the year included a new mangle for ironing, new lighting for the studio and offices, the purchase of a commercial refrigerator, and a survey of the heating and ventilation systems. Many small enhancements to operations were made as well. Class schedules were printed in booklet form to better inform existing members and provide another tool for recruiting new ones. A bylaws change established that 10 percent of the resident members attending any special or annual meeting would constitute a quorum.

The Entertainment Trustee had five busy committees—Hospitality, Tea, Bridge, Dance, and Ballroom Dancing—as well as three special committees—Stunt Night, Birthday Party, and Trustee Breakfast. Dance classes enrolled 270 children of members and nonmembers, netting $534 in the first year. Given their increasing popularity, these classes became an important source

Bertha Knight Landes was a woman for all seasons. A charter member of the Women's University Club, she was also a member of the Woman's Century Club and the League of Women Voters, as well as a devoted wife and mother and an excellent homemaker.

She won a seat on the Seattle City Council in 1922 and became the first woman council president in 1924. Her husband said that civic office "is simply a natural enlargement of her sphere . . . there's no difference between running one home and a hundred thousand."

In 1926, she ran for mayor, vowing, "If elected Mayor, I promise to wage a relentless warfare on all crooks, thieves, bandits, burglars, stick-up men and other law-defying characters." She defeated the incumbent, Doc Brown, by a margin of 6,000 votes. Hers was an honest, clean, and capable administration. She was the first woman mayor of a major U.S. city, and the only woman mayor that Seattle has ever had. Although she was endorsed for reelection in 1928 by all the city's major newspapers, the Central Labor Council, the Prohibition Party, and many women's groups, she lost to Frank Edwards, an outcome she attributed primarily to "sex prejudice."

Her leadership continued in other organizations. She was the first woman moderator of Washington's Conference of Congregational and Christian Churches and national president of the American Federation of Soroptimist Clubs. She and her husband led University of Washington–sponsored study groups to the Far East from 1933 to 1936, and in the summer after his death, she led the tour alone. In 1934, she gave two lectures at the Women's University Club, "Civic Structure" and "City Government and Women's Role."

Mrs. Landes died in 1943 at the age of seventy-five. This remarkable woman is well-remembered for her many accomplishments. A conference room in Seattle City Hall is named in her honor.

In December 1933, as Hitler took power in Germany, Rose Glass reviewed three books about Germany: Germany Enters the Third Reich *by Calvin B. Hoover;* My Battle (Mein Kampf) *by Adolf Hitler; and* The Brown Book of the Hitler Terror and the Burning of the Reichstag *by the World Committee for the Victims of German Fascism. Other books reviewed in 1933-34 included* The Bulpington of Blup *by H. G. Wells;* Lost Horizon *by James Hilton;* English Journey *by J. B. Priestley, and a biography of Marie Antoinette.*

Bulletins (December 1933–December 1934)

The beautiful grandfather clock in the entrance hall was made by William McEwan of Auchterarder, Scotland, in the 1790s. It was purchased with donations from members in 1937 in memory of Dr. Mabel Seagrave, a founding member of the WUC. She served in France in World War I, was the guiding force behind the building of the clubhouse in 1922, and was active in the Club until her death.

Two important founding members died in 1935.

Dr. Seagrave Dies While At Sunday Dinner

DR. MABEL SEAGRAVE
—McBride & Anderson Photo

Funeral services for Dr. Mabel

MRS. BACKUS IS TAKEN BY DEATH

Mrs. Edith Helen Fredericka Backus, wife of Leroy M. Backus, real estate operator and capitalist, died yesterday afternoon at their home in The Highlands after two years' illness. Mrs. Backus, born in New York and a graduate of Columbia University, came to Seattle in 1898, and since then had been a leader in Seattle society. She founded the Women's University Club and the Seattle Day Nursery, and for years was an active member of the Seattle Garden Club. She was a member of the Dutch Reform Church.

Mrs. Leroy M. Backus

Her husband is the son of Man... F. Backus, pioneer Seattle ...ker, who died last February. ...he family has made tentative ...s for funeral services Tuesday ...r the direction of Bonney-...n.

...des her husband, Mrs. Backus ...ived by two daughters, Mrs. ...raddy of San Pedro, Calif., ...s Edith Marjorie Backus ...le; three sons, Manson F. ...nd, Walter Clinton Backus ...y M. Backus, Jr.

of Club revenue and remained so for many years. Plans were also made for evening activities in which "young married women as well as members who are employed during the day will be most cordially included."

In the summer of 1937, the 230 members of Book Review held their annual picnic at the summer home of Marion Mesdag (Mrs. Tom) at Three Tree Point. The Broadmoor Garden Party, featuring bridge games and tea, was held on July 21—"that famous day of ours on which the rain has never fallen in Seattle," the *Bulletin* noted.

Another successful event took place for the first time on October 25, 1937. The *Bulletin* announced the details:

> *A Continental Dinner! A new innovation for the Club, and what a thrilling one it sounds to be—friendly, gay, and cosmopolitan . . . Bring your escort. Dinner at seven, $1.25/person.*

Afterward, the Entertainment Trustee reported to the board: "The Continental Dinner Dance was such a success that it was suggested another be planned for December." The theme for this dance was "Christmas in Merrie England," and attendees sang English tunes and carols accompanied by an orchestra. "Diners came at 7 o'clock and stayed to wear the evening away on twinkling toes. And what light the candles didn't shed, the flaming plum pudding did," the *Seattle Times* reported on December 17, 1937.

The same month, 200 women attended an unusual Book Review event featuring a history of the Northwest, *Beyond the Shining Mountains*, written by Dorothy Fay Gould, a University of Washington professor. Pictures were shown on a stereopticon machine (an early slide projector) for an hour and a half.

> *"In serving you we are helping the club, for such work keeps the kitchen busy during the slack season. . . . It hardly pays for you to do your own cooking during the summer months."*
>
> *Bulletin (June 1937)*

CATERING DEPARTMENT

CAKES—

Two-layer Cake (Iced)	$1.00
One-layer Cake (Iced)	.50
(This cake will cut 25 tea squares)	
Large Round Birthday Cake	2.00
Angel Food Cake (iced)	.90
Indv. Sunshine Rings, doz.	.60
Indv. Reception Cakes, doz.	.60
(Iced in pastel colors)	
Pecan Dainties and Cocoanut Snow Balls, doz.	.60
(Not less than 5 doz.)	

PIES—

Fruit or Cream	.50
Mince	.60
George Washington	.60
Indv. Cream Pie, doz.	1.20

SANDWICHES and ROLLS—

Assorted Open Face, doz.	.45
Closed (Full Size), doz.	1.20
Chicken (Full Size), each	.20
Finger Rolls, doz.	.20
Parker House, doz.	.25
Cinnamon or Butterscotch, doz.	.30
Toast Cases, doz.	.75
(A discount of 10% on all orders over 5 doz.)	

COOKIES—

Small Ice Box, doz.	.15
Small Chocolate, doz.	.15
Fudge Squares, doz.	.30

DELICATESSEN—

Chicken Cutlets, doz.	1.50
Crab Cutlets, doz.	1.25
Chicken Salad (mostly chicken), pt.	1.00
Chow Mein (serves 6 or 8)	1.75
Chow Mein (with Mandarin Sauce)	2.00
Chocolate, Caramel or Butterscotch Sauce, qt.	.80
Mayonnaise (in your own container), pt.	.30
French Dressing (in your own container), pt.	.20
Roasting and Stuffing a Turkey, Goose or Duck	2.50

(One day's NOTICE required on Catering Orders)

Sandwiches, hot entrées, and beverages by the gallon were available from the Club's catering department for easy summertime entertaining.

Fredericka Shaw, 1937 Club president, was photographed wearing the couture fashions noted by local reporters. "I think it is the duty of every feminine leader, every clubwoman to be well-dressed," she said.

Mrs. Gordon Shaw Gives Hints For Wardrobe

We talked to Mrs. Gordon Shaw the other day and found that a smart and important lady was voting for a smart and important style. Mrs. Shaw, president of the Women's University Club, has ample reason to know what the smartly dressed clubwoman's wardrobe can and should do for her, and we were interested to know how Mrs. Shaw always manages to look so well and so appropriately dressed despite her many activities.

Said Mrs. Shaw: "I find the dress and coat ensemble the most satisfactory for general wear, though the simple tailored suit worn with furs is very appropriate when attending book reviews or things of that type."

The coat and dress ensemble, or costume suit, is a boon to any busy woman's wardrobe. Suitable for

HEADS WOMEN'S 'U' CLUB

...ent of the Women's University ...nine leader, every clubwoman ...one of the new small off-the-...silver fox scarfs with a black ...nard Fink.)

Fall Styles Hold Eyes Of Women At Display

No, Mr. Pitkin, with all due respect—and apologies for harping on an old theme—life does not necessarily begin at forty, for women, anyway. It begins all over again every fall, when fashion shows form the height of entertainment at all gatherings.

Yesterday, while members of the Women's University Club and their guests munched cinnamon toast and dropped a lemon slice in their teacups, life began again with a bang. The old life of navy sheers, candy-striped organdies, leghorn hats with streamers, figured crepe jacket frocks, was slipping away. The new, vital life of gray and brown woolly suits with clever fastenings, of slick black satin frocks, of luscious, trailing velvet gowns, of knobby little felt hats with crisp veils, had its beginning.

The fashion parade, put on by a Seattle shop, began after guests were greeted by Mrs. Donald True-

HOSTESSES FOR JUNIORS

When sons and daughters of Women's University Club members entertain with a 6:30 o'clock dinner and dancing party Friday evening, December 28, at the club, these girls will be hostesses: (Back row, left to right) Misses Jeanette Lewis, Barbara Lamping and Marian Matthias; (front row, left to right) Misses Agnes Shaw, Betty Shaw, Margaret Macpherson and Barbara Shank.

Hostesses for one of the monthly junior dance classes

Elsie Savidge hosted one of the Summer Bridge Teas offered in Broadmoor homes in July 1937.

Hostess

Mrs. S. Leigh Savidge, who will be hostess at her beautiful home in Broadmoor Wednesday afternoon for the tea hour following bridge parties in twelve Broadmoor homes. The affair will be given by the Women's University Club.

The year 1938 began with such a whirlwind of social activities and classes that one wag on the board feared the *Bulletin* was becoming "so voluminous that before long it will assume to proportions of a magazine." Four hundred members attended the New Year's Day Open House for supper, with bridge in the Library and card room. Dancing took place in the downstairs auditorium, and socializing in the Drawing Room. All the festivities were illuminated by candlelight.

Monday Evening Group—a favorite of Club residents and members who were unavailable for daytime classes and events—added an active program of badminton and ping-pong to its agenda of activities, making use of the auditorium. The badminton court stayed open until 11:15 P.M. each Monday and was reserved for the exclusive use of the group. The *Seattle Sunday Times* reported that Monday's popular informal buffet dinners were "the stimulus for the formation of groups in tap dancing, horseback riding, glove making, wood carving and the drama."

Cultural programs abounded. The revived Handbag Players presented *A Bohemian Night at the Theater,* with an ethnic-themed supper served before the play. Their other plays included a thrilling murder mystery, a specialty act, and a one-act comedy. In a high point of the 1938 Book Review season, Eleanor Roosevelt's autobiography, *This Is My Story,* was reviewed by Roosevelt's daughter, Anna Boettiger, editor of the *Seattle Post-Intelligencer* women's page.

The start of the Spanish Civil War in 1936 and Japan's invasion of China in 1937 gave new urgency to current affairs. Two leaders from the Chinese Women's Club of Shanghai, as well as businessman W. E. Priestly, spoke on the events in China. Members organized a "listener club," which gathered around the radio for *America's Town Meeting of the Air,* a show on ABC featuring noted national figures conversing about public affairs, and then discussed the topic themselves.

In spite of the dark clouds hovering over Asia and Europe, the thirties ended with an extraordinary event celebrating the Club's twenty-fifth anniversary: Eleanor Roosevelt spoke at a Club dinner on March 27, 1939.

The announcement in the *Bulletin* reflected how significant the event was to members:

> *Rarely, if ever, has the Club had as a guest speaker one who plays such a prominent role in contemporary American history. The event is even more striking to us as members of the Women's University Club, because that person is a woman and because we must fully appreciate that in the eyes of historians, Mrs. Franklin D. Roosevelt will live as one of the most influential women in American history.*

Years later, President Edith Carlson (Mrs. Paul) remembered: "The high point in our year was the evening when Mrs. Roosevelt was our guest. The distinction of our guest and the distinction of our audience composed exclusively of Club members, made what we shall always remember as a brilliant occasion."

Throughout the 1930s, the Club held itself to the highest standards in conducting business and providing a unique, stimulating, and culturally diverse setting for its members. The perseverance and inventive thinking of the Depression years demonstrated to future members the way to do their best in all circumstances. These qualities would be put to the test in the years to come.

Speaker's Dinner
in honor of
Mrs. Franklin D. Roosevelt
Masonic University Club - March 27, 1939 -

First Lady, In Seattle, Tells Of Her Mail

Everywhere that Mrs. Franklin D. Roosevelt goes, that bulging mail bag is sure to follow. She can't get away from it, for if she once takes a week's vacation without those letters from every part of the country, those letters that tell her what America is thinking and doing, she will have a mountainous pile of them on her desk when she gets back to the White House.

So, on train and airplane, in the White House, her New York apartment and the homes of her children, those letters are opened and answered by someone—by the government agency which covers certain appeals, by the secretary, or by the First Lady, herself.

And, Mrs. Roosevelt told members of the Women's University Club, before whom she spoke last evening after a dinner in her honor, she wouldn't have given up the opportunity she has had, since 1933, to know the country and its people, that has come to her through these letters.

Some Funny, Some Pathetic

Some of them are funny, some are pathetic, many are critical and many flattering, a number are full of plans to solve the nation's problems—but all of them are perused carefully.

"I wouldn't have it any different," she said. "I have learned so much. Before I went to the White House, I used to read a great deal of fiction. Now my reading matter is in the mail—only it isn't fiction. It is real life, it is real drama, real tragedy, real comedy or real success. It is the greatest picture of the United States."

First Lady Eleanor Roosevelt addressed a well-attended dinner given in her honor by the Women's University Club.

Newspaper artists' sketch of WUC facade

This Red Cross clubmobile will be completely outfitted with recreational facilities by the Women's University Club for the amusement of soldiers in Alaska. Funds for its equipment came from the tea and the sale of the club's cookbook. Miss Dorothy Torp, staff assistant, military welfare division, American Red Cross, is at the wheel. Others are (left to right) Mr. Sherman Sanders, assistant field director for the Red Cross; Mrs. Arthur E. Simon and Mrs. Stanley D. Lyle, who poured at the tea.—All pictures on this page by Harold Smith, Seattle Times photographer.

Chapter 4

Weathering the War Years

ON SEPTEMBER 1, 1939, GERMANY INVADED POLAND; ENGLAND AND FRANCE declared war. Although the United States initially remained neutral, it became more and more difficult to ignore events in Europe and Asia. In this atmosphere, Club leaders attempted to maintain a positive attitude and an air of calm. At the September 26 board meeting, the Literature and Art Trustee asked how her committees should proceed during the international

crisis. The board decided "the committees [should] follow the policy of having the political and war situations confined to classes and Town Meetings, and the luncheon and dinner speakers chosen from the field of the arts."

The war captured members' attention, however, with talks such as "The Powder Keg of Europe," delivered by Oliver Haskell at the World Trends Program in December. The February 1940 Travel Talk, "Afghanistan: The Buffer Between Communist Russia and British-Controlled India," featured one of the few Americans to penetrate Afghanistan, Mrs. Laurence Peterson, who gave an illustrated lecture about crossing that country with her husband in a Ford truck. Keenly aware of the interest in current events, the board and Speakers Committee joined forces at the Club's Birthday Party in February 1940 to present the gift of a new radio for the *America's Town Meeting of the Air* broadcasts.

That year, Stunt Night provided a welcome diversion from wartime news. "Broadcasts from Station WUC" featured skits performed by members of the Book Review class, Drama class, Club Orchestra, Chorus, and Monday Evening Group. Audience members were invited to come costumed as their favorite radio stars, such as Fibber McGee and Molly.

By the time of the May Annual Meeting in 1940, the Club had much to be grateful for. In addition to a new staff team, led by Club manager Grace Ballinger, the Club had $8,545 in the bank and $2,226 set aside for bond retirement. All rooms on the second and third floors had been washed or redecorated, the kitchen had been completely remodeled with a new ventilation system and stainless steel tops on all the stations, and a new front entrance canopy had been purchased. Sadly, Anna Trefethen, a Club founder and its fifth president, passed away that year.

Less than two weeks after Margretta Hillman (Mrs. R. Kline) took office as president, the British evacuated Dunkirk; within a month, Germany had occupied Paris. On June 26, 1940, under the headline "Red Cross Women Write Hymn of Human Kindness," Virginia Boren wrote in the *Seattle Daily Times*, "The favorite occupation of Seattle society today is knitting, stitching, cutting for the American Red Cross." In August, the Red Cross announced that the Women's University Club was to be one of the units in the city to do surgical dressing work.

Presidents	
Margretta Hillman	*1940–41*
Ruth Peterson	*1941–42*
Edna Vaupell	*1942–43*
Victoria Simon	*1943–44*
Leah McKay	*1944–45*
Maud May	*1945–46*
Agnes Smith	*1946–47*
Inez Bowden	*1947–48*
Agnes Crosby	*1948–49*
Dorothy Cassill	*1949–50*

🦎 In the News

June 5, 1940	Lake Washington Floating Bridge opens, connecting Seattle with Mercer Island and the Eastside
November 7, 1940	Tacoma Narrows Bridge "Galloping Gertie" collapses
October 20, 1941	Sir Thomas Beecham becomes conductor of the Seattle Symphony
December 7, 1941	Japan attacks Pearl Harbor; U.S. declares war
April 21, 1942	Japanese Americans are ordered to evacuate Seattle; more than 12,000 leave King County
May 8, 1945	Germany surrenders; Victory in Europe Day
August 15, 1945	Japan surrenders; World War II ends
November 2, 1948	Harry Truman defeats Thomas Dewey for president
April 13, 1949	A 7.1-magnitude earthquake kills seven people in Seattle
July 9,1949	Seattle-Tacoma International Airport opens

THEIR TEA SERVED WITH A VIEW

After their annual summer bridge event, members and guests met for afternoon tea in the Laurelhurst lakeside garden of Nelle Cowan.

*M*argretta Hillman's year as president was a busy one. Kenneth Callahan, the well-known artist and curator at the Seattle Art Museum, exhibited his work in the card room during July 1940. The Traditional Events Committee presented its usual year's worth of fare, including the New Year's Day Open House, Club Birthday Party (February), Presidents' Reception (spring), Trustees' Annual Luncheon (May), Summer Tea (July), Family Tree Luncheon (August), and Autumn Brunch (September). Programs and speakers continued to reflect events in the world at large. Mary Ashby Cheek, president of Rockford College, discussed being constructive in an age of destruction. A speaker on *America's Town Meeting of the Air* posed the question "Should the English-speaking world unite now?" A few weeks later, a Fireside Talk focused on "The German Occupation of France."

For the second year in a row, the Special Finance Committee announced at the Annual Meeting that Club finances were stronger than ever. With this in mind, Mrs. Hillman proposed repealing the "special emergency measure"—adopted in the 1930s—that permitted women to join the Club without paying an initiation fee, and proposed returning to an initiation fee of $50. In the fall of 1941, members overwhelmingly approved both proposals, and the board dedicated the income from initiation fees to retiring bonds and maintaining the clubhouse.

With an eye toward increasing members' participation, Mrs. Hillman reorganized the structure of several committees. The president assumed responsibility for appointing new members each year, thus ending the practice of members serving permanently or choosing their friends to succeed them. This allowed the membership of the Corporate Finance and Permanent Decorating Committees to be completely renewed every five years, and the Library Committee every three. Mrs. Hillman was also the first to propose a systematic effort to preserve the history and traditions of the Club.

On December 7, 1941, Japan attacked Pearl Harbor: the United States was suddenly at war. At its regular meeting two days later, the board decided to continue with Club operations, making whatever adjustments might be necessary due to blackouts or war emergencies. Club residents immediately met to formulate plans in case of air raids. Approximately $7,000 was spent on repairs and replacements and $1,000 to purchase new fixtures to make sure the Club would have "adequate supplies to meet any emergency." By May, the Club stood ready to black out all the rooms and bathrooms upstairs and all

AVIS IMPORTANT!
"La classe de francais [sic] commencera un nouveau livre, le 5 Janvier 1940. C'est le moment de joindre cette classe si hautement interessante."

Bulletin (January 1940)

"ANGELS OF MERCY"— Mrs. Robert P. Judy (left) and Mrs. Robert D. McAusland, headed the dis play of Red Cross work at the club's opening event. This exhibit shows the knitting and bandage rolling done in Red Cross classes, also the first-aid courses offered. Miss Gale Guthrie, talented artist, made the posters for the exhibit.—Sketches by Parker McAllister, Seattle Times staff artist.

Each fall, the Autumn Breakfast event showcased the broad variety of classes and activities scheduled for the coming year. The display of the Club's Red Cross work presaged the active involvement that was to begin on December 7, 1941.

U.S. Treasury citation in recognition of Club war bond sales

World War II Club Members in Service

Red Cross
Mildred Boyle
Genevieve Gay
Patricia Hughes
Elaine Jensen
Rosemary Langheldt
Katherine McCollister
Elizabeth Pitt

Marine Corps
Barbara Berens
Janice Crowder
Jean Louise Miller
Mary Adelaide Moran
Ruth Pearce
Willye White

WACs
Elizabeth Duncan
Norma Fritz
Kay Marilley
Frances Sutcliffe

WAVES
Kate Chittenden
Mary Ann Fleetwood
Kay Garland
Betty Ann Hollander
Jane Horsfall
Maxine Neitz
Jeannette Uddenberg

World War II was a defining moment in the lives of a generation. Women's University Club members took an active part in every aspect of the war effort, giving generously of their time, energy, and money. Twenty-four Club members served overseas; many more served on the home front. Still others, such as Ada Belle Wood (Mrs. Paul E.), worked in war industries, proud to be counted as a colleague of Rosie the Riveter. Each job, here or there, big or small, exemplified the spirit of sharing, the very essence of the Club.

Member Rosemary Langheldt was stationed with the Red Cross in England. A member of the Club's Creative Writing class, she later turned a family collection of her letters home into a book, *Dearest Ones: A True World War II Love Story*. Writing on October 20, 1944, she described the difficulties of getting around in London during the blackout: "After seeing Piccadilly Circus in full midnight bloom, I think I understand better the Brits' favorite lament . . . 'The Yanks are overpaid, oversexed, and over here.'" On January 27, 1945, she wrote a more sober reflection to her family:

> . . . *the 2,000,000th Yank embarked from this Port on the sixteenth, with appropriate ceremonies. Similar to those held for the 1,000,000th Yank . . . last October, that shy young private from Pennsylvania. I still see him standing halfway up the gangway, very embarrassed as the British and American brass singled him out and presented him with a new mess kit. . . . We just heard that he was killed six weeks after he landed in France. I sure hope this guy has better luck.*"

At home, the Club and the Red Cross were allies in arms. Designated as a local unit for surgical dressing work, the clubhouse served as headquarters for Red Cross and civilian defense groups. Classes in first aid and surgical dressing met there regularly. Neither training nor experience was required, just a white apron and a square of cambric for a head covering. The goal was 500,000 bandages per month.

Although the Clubmobiles financed by cookbook sales were the most visible of the Club's projects to support the troops, members took on dozens of other tasks, such as collecting books, cartons of cigarettes, and small comfort kits for the Red Cross. On New Year's Day 1944, thirty members assembled and wrapped 1,024 packages. New and used yarn was available at the Club each Wednesday; knitting afghan squares for the Red Cross in Book Review class was encouraged.

The Club did not overlook needs close to home. One of the most important wartime jobs in Seattle was that of providing care for children of mothers working in war industries. When day nurseries were opened in public schools, the chairman of the Club's War Projects Committee, Orpha McAusland (Mrs. Robert D.), announced that the Club would furnish equipment for them.

Tireless sorting and transporting of items to furnish over 500 rooms for the Coast Guard in the area was the contribution of members Ruth Peterson (Mrs. Sterling D.), Virginia Baldwin (Mrs. Wilden H.), and Irvina Pratt (Mrs. Henry P.).

In 1945, to the tunes of "The White Cliffs of Dover," "Comin' In on a Wing and a Prayer," "Ac-Cent-Tchu-Ate the Positive," and "Stardust," members joined all Americans in celebrating V-E Day (May 8) and V-J Day (August 15). The Club had carried on. Volunteerism had enhanced the lives of those who served and those who were served.

> *"Making Surgical Dressings? Knitting? Comfort kits? Also, think of signing up for Home Hospitality—what servicemen need is the informal atmosphere of the average home for dinner or over night. Fill out the enclosed form."*
>
> Bulletin (November 1942)

On March 31, 1942, Stunt Night revived the first presentation, staged by Willye White in 1917 during World War I. Using the original cast, costumes, and skits saved not only money but valuable rehearsal time "because women are too busy with defense and war work."

—Official U. S. N. Photo.
LIEUTENANT (j. g.) FRANCES RICH, U. S. N. R.

Reporter Mary Coyle Osmun noted the new look of a speaker who came to the Club on April 7, 1943, Lieutenant Frances Rich: "There were 160 women at the Women's University Club yesterday to hear Lieutenant Rich speak at the luncheon and every one of them would have been proud to have her for a daughter.... By choice, Frances Rich wears her curly hair cropped short, the most becoming hair arrangement possible with the turned up Wave hat. Except for a little pink lipstick her face is devoid of make-up. Her nails are cut short and bare of polish. She doesn't smoke. She looks and acts like the lady she is from her training and education and like the 'gentleman' she is, as an officer in the United States Navy."

—*Seattle Times*, April 8, 1943

BIRTHDAY PARTY APRIL 9
One of Our Special Club Days!
"This year, let us bring our personal gifts to our boys in the services. A good book, a carton of cigarettes, or anything else the boys would like. Make it a real birthday gift from our hearts."

Bulletin (March 1943)

"Miss Whitehead has come to tell us how to amuse sailors."

essential rooms downstairs. All forty-four guest rooms were filled to capacity, and the Club was serving over 4,300 meals each month.

With the clubhouse and its residents secure, the board swung into action. A War Projects Committee was formed; dues of members serving in the armed forces were waived; and the Club bought war bonds in its own name and sold them to members. Whenever enough money accumulated in checking or savings accounts, the board purchased another war bond. The Club received a U.S. Treasury citation for sale of government bonds during the first and third bond drives. By 1945, bonds credited to the Women's University Club totaled $602,025.

Recalling the first Stunt Night as "a cessation from worry during the trying days of the last war," Willye White assembled her original cast to stage a complete revival of the show—with the same acts, the same costumes, and the same women. Headlines from the notices in the March 1917 *Bulletin* appeared again in March 1942: "Everybody come to Stunt Night. . . . Be prepared to sing all the new war songs: 'K-K-K-Katy,' 'Over There,' 'Pack Up Your Troubles' . . . and many others. Come in costumes of 1917 and come prepared to put on a stunt. Come prepared to give your all!"

Looking for ways to be of service beyond their Red Cross work, Club members hit on an idea that began quietly enough—a County Fair to which members could bring hobbies, handicrafts, and flowers for sale, with proceeds to benefit the war effort. One of the highlights was a Cookies for Rookies contest, with prizes awarded for the best submissions. Hundreds of leftover cookies, along with books and magazines, were sent to servicemen's clubs.

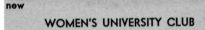

new

WOMEN'S UNIVERSITY CLUB

COOKBOOK
Treasured Recipes of Seattle

It is hot off the griddle, skillet and press.

Of course you've been working for years on the theory that "the way to a man's heart is through his stomach," but haven't you run into some detours? The same old food cooked and served in the same old way and pretty soon you're a wall-flower wife! Are you guilty of still feeding your husband the identical oatmeal cookies that your college son teethed on? Are you weary of trying to change the personality of a carrot? Does your family complain that all your meats taste like "ROAST BEAST" without any distinguishing flavor?

Advertisement for the Club's first cookbook, available in January 1943 for $1.25 per copy, tax included. Handwritten recipes and "fascinating bits of local history" illustrated with sketches of Seattle enlivened the pages. All proceeds supported the War Projects Fund. (*Bulletin*, December 1942)

The success of the cookie contest and the frequent requests for copies of the recipes gave birth to the idea of creating and selling a cookbook. Members contributed recipes, and the House and Garden Group put the book together. The first printing of 2,000 copies sold briskly enough to make the cookbook project a major source of funding for the Club's war projects, the most visible of which was the furnishing of three Clubmobiles—Red Cross service clubs on wheels supplied with canteens, books, magazines, and the latest music—for servicemen posted in Alaska and the Aleutians.

By the time of its second printing, the Club's cookbook had to take into account the realities of government rationing of sugar, meat, and dozens of other foodstuffs, resulting in a special addendum of substitutes for rationed items. Sugar rationing forced the board to reduce service of the Club's famous pecan rolls to three days a week. When Irma Rombauer, the author of *Joy of Cooking*, spoke to the Monday Evening Group on August 30, 1943, the *Seattle Times* quoted her at length: "At long last cooking has taken its place among the Arts. Cooks have become important. Women past 60 years of age are flocking to cooking schools and sophisticated socialites are eager to learn how to make gravy." The *Times* further observed: "Mrs. Rombauer's book has had a phenomenal success due, she modestly states, to the fact that many families have been deprived of their cooks and women are looking for short-cuts and simple ways of preparing and serving meals without sacrificing standards."

By August 1943, it was getting hard to keep staff, and even harder to feed members. The board decided that ration points must be used for dinner parties of more than four, unless fish or chicken was ordered. By the end of 1943, the staffing situation had become a constant worry for the board. The dining room manager left to get married and could not be replaced, leaving the Club manager, Grace Ballinger, to do both jobs.

At the thirty-fourth Birthday Party, Leah McKay accepted a citation presented to the Club by Captain H. V. Hughes from the 13th Naval District "in grateful acknowledgement of exceptional cooperation and outstanding services rendered to the Medical Department of the Navy during the period of World War II." Mrs. McKay was president in 1944–45.

The housing shortages of the war years meant that by the fall of 1943, there was a waiting list for the upstairs bedrooms. Housekeeping became more difficult because "the labor situation makes it impossible to keep up as we would like." And there was no chance of making major improvements. Under the circumstances, it was a victory just to keep the building clean and in repair.

The Club's longtime cooperation with the all-male College Club, which had relocated to the southeast corner of Sixth and Spring when the Club moved to the northwest corner, continued to prosper. During the war years, the two clubs traded ration points and tried to schedule large dinners at different times, to give each Club a better chance to obtain the needed supplies. When the Women's University Club

A song composed for 1943 Stunt Night

Welcome to the U. Club Canteen
Are you a WAAC or a WAVE,
A gob or a mighty marine?
Are you a flyer or soldier?
Then come to the U. Club Canteen.

Are you a ship-yard worker,
Putting sub in a submarine?
Are you a welder at Boeing's?
Well, come to the U. Club Canteen.

Are you a poor home defenser,
Saving your last coffee bean?
Are you a weary Air Raiden?
Then come to the U. Club Canteen.

Do you want to see Power and Gable,
Garbo, Lamarr and Marlene?
Do you want to watch movie stars twinkle?
Then come to the U. Club Canteen.

Do you want to step out and be gay?
Do you want to see and be seen
At the "Hottest Spot" in Seattle?
Well, come to the U. Club Canteen.

Bulletin (March 1943)

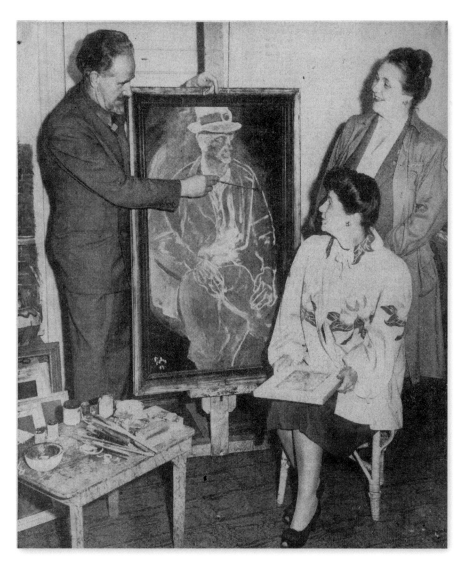

Mark Tobey, a nationally known
Pacific Northwest artist, taught
Club art classes in his studio.
Observing Tobey critiquing one
of his recent paintings are student
painters Fay Nicholson (seated)
and Mrs. F. G. Carpenter.

had overflow crowds for special dinner programs, those who could not be accommodated in the dining room ate at the College Club across the street and returned for the program—and the system worked in reverse for the men's group. Because the College Club had a liquor license and the Women's University Club did not, members wishing to entertain with before-dinner cocktails could often do so at the men's club.

In spite of war work and staffing difficulties, the Club's menu of classes and programs continued in full swing. In 1943, Stunt Night welcomed Club members to the "U. Club Canteen." During the year, speakers discussed every aspect of the world situation, from China's role as an ally to American relief for Norway. The Summer Tea became another fund-raiser for the war effort.

The impact of war was hard to miss at the May 1944 Annual Meeting. Gas rationing made it difficult to collect flowers from members' homes for decorating the Club. For the same reason, the Linens Committee could not meet, which left just two members to do the huge amount of repair and mending required. Due to the shortage of gas, committee work was accomplished by phone.

Through all these difficulties, the close friendships forged at the Club played an important role in supporting members whose brothers, fiancés, husbands, or friends were at the front. Victoria Simon (Mrs. Arthur E.), the 1943–44 president, felt the Club should be a haven and refuge for members, as they were in turn "morale builders" for the wartime community. Small victories, such as keeping the dining room open for three meals a day, seven days a week, in spite of staff shortages and food rationing, were in her view a critical part of the Club's war work and its effort to "keep the home fires burning."

At the May 1945 Annual Meeting, eight days after Germany surrendered, President Leah McKay (Mrs. William O.) said it best: "We began the year in a spirit of humility with the will to face each day as it came. We wished the Club to be a pleasant, joyous place in which those with heavy sorrows and those who were tired from their war work could refresh their spirits and gain new courage from association with their friends."

Influential leaders gathered for the thirty-fifth anniversary of the Club's incorporation. Left to right: Ruth Peterson (1941), Willye White (1924), Wilma Norris, Laura Carr (1921), Alvilde Clark (1925). All except Mrs. Peterson were 1914 charter members. (Dates indicate year of presidency.)

MADAME PRESIDENTS: Mrs. Will G. Crosby (left), president of the Women's University Club, and Mrs. Florence Denny Heliker, oldest living former president. Mrs. Heliker, who was president in 1916, is a daughter of the late Mr. Rolland H. Denny, who was 2½ months old when he arrived at Alki Point with his parents, Mr. and Mrs. A. A. Denny, on the schooner Exact in 1851. Mrs. Heliker is sitting beside a chest which she helped give to the club.

Celebrating history at the Club's thirty-fifth Birthday Party were president Agnes Crosby, left, and Florence Heliker, the oldest living former president, who served in 1916. Mrs. Heliker was a daughter of Roland H. Denny, who arrived at Alki Point with his parents, Mr. and Mrs. A. A. Denny, in 1851. She is seated next to an antique chest that she helped to purchase for the Club.

Even after the war ended, its effects lingered: although most soldiers came home, many remained in hospitals in the Northwest and elsewhere. In response, the Club's War Projects Committee became the Rehabilitation Committee, working through the Camp and Hospital Committee of the Red Cross. It focused on the needs of hospitalized vets, providing symphony tickets and small comforts. The Knitting Committee reported that it had produced twenty-one Army and Navy sweaters, twenty garments for French children, and forty afghan squares. A request from the VA hospital to invite small groups of six or eight servicemen to some of the lectures at the Club was approved by the board.

The Rehabilitation Committee continued to be alert to the needs of veterans for several years, including gathering stamps for bedridden vets who might be interested in stamp collecting. (President Roosevelt had been an avid collector.) They continued the successful cookbook project to support programs at Fort Lawton and the Naval Hospital in Bremerton and recommended purchasing 100 sets of earphones at a cost of $250 as a gift to the Marine Hospital in Seattle, which the board quickly approved.

Well-earned recognition was received in 1948, when Leah McKay, who served as president during 1944–45, accepted a Navy citation for the "noteworthy contributions of the Club during the war years."

During the 1946 Annual Meeting, members approved numerous amendments to the bylaws reflecting changes the war had brought—growth of membership but also growth of the community. For example, the geographic area used to determine a member's status as "resident" was expanded from within a twenty-five-mile radius of Pioneer Square to within a fifty-mile radius. More changes were made to committee structures, and a number of standing committees were added. This postwar world required fresh ideas, and the Club was getting organized to move forward with confidence.

The toll on the building and furnishings from years of heavy use and deferred maintenance also required action. In July, the board authorized installation of a dumbwaiter and the development of architectural plans and estimates for a variety of improvements to

"The smart, good-looking woman at 1105 Sixth Av., who is celebrating her 35th birthday, is fast-approaching middle life, but instead of being ashamed of her age, she's happy and telling about it and getting smarter, better looking and younger every day. 'She' is the Women's University Club, which this month is commemorating the 35th anniversary of its incorporation."

Seattle Times, February 20, 1949

the lavatories, studio, ventilation, kitchen equipment, and storage. Several projects had already been authorized. The Permanent Decorating Committee proceeded with brightening the halls, redecorating the powder room, installing better lighting, and doing "everything else they can do to make our Club a pleasant and restful place in which to meet." Room 317 was designated as the Board Room, also to be available for use by residents for a parlor and by committees for meetings, to free up the main floor for social uses. In all, the board allocated $20,000 for Club improvements.

Although events on the world stage remained important, members were finally at liberty to give more attention to matters at home. Anticipating the postwar housing boom, Mr. J. J. Chiarelli, a prominent Seattle architect, spoke on "New Houses and Houses Made New." Humor ruled as local author Betty MacDonald spoke about her best-selling book *The Egg and I.* Reviews of Frank Gilbreth's *Cheaper by the Dozen* and Betty Smith's *A Tree Grows in Brooklyn* captivated the Book Review class.

The newspapers returned to the kind of society page reporting they had featured before the war, although shortages of newsprint limited the amount of coverage they could supply for a time. After so many years of sacrifice, members were more than ready to return to the days of glorious garden parties. In August 1946, the Summer Tea—which entailed transporting all the dishes, food, tables, and sun umbrellas to the Windermere homes of neighboring Club members—was, in the words of the Entertainment Chairman, "a beautiful party and an outstanding success as was shown by the attendance of 458 persons." The daughters of members helped to serve.

Soon after the war ended, the Club also reinstated the popular (and profitable) dance classes for junior high and high school students. The junior high classes focused on learning to dance. The Sophomore Smoothies for high school sophomores and the Galadears for juniors and seniors offered dances along with demonstrations of the latest steps. The Galadears were even photographed for *Seventeen* magazine in the early fifties, though the board would not allow the Club's name to be used to identify them.

Evidence of the war in daily life was fading from view by the beginning of 1949. There were occasional aid requests for reconstruction projects (e.g., candles were collected at the front desk and melted down for reuse in "Europe's darkened homes, schools and churches"), and books were collected and donated to the Red Cross. As the decade ended, the Club's membership and finances had increased twofold, with a long list of prospective members waiting to join and a short list of outstanding debts.

Slowly but surely, members were moving forward into a kind of normalcy not known for nearly twenty years. The challenges of the Depression and war—successfully met with hope, creativity, and cooperative effort—established a strong foundation as the Club prepared to embrace the second half of the twentieth century.

The Galadears were a hugely popular dance group for high school juniors and seniors. Dance cards, waiting to be filled by a variety of partners, were a favorite feature of each event.

> *"Make sure your sons in Smoothies and Galadears are asking girls to dance. Opportunities for unfavorable conduct occur when your son DOES NOT dance."*
>
> Bulletin (January 1954)

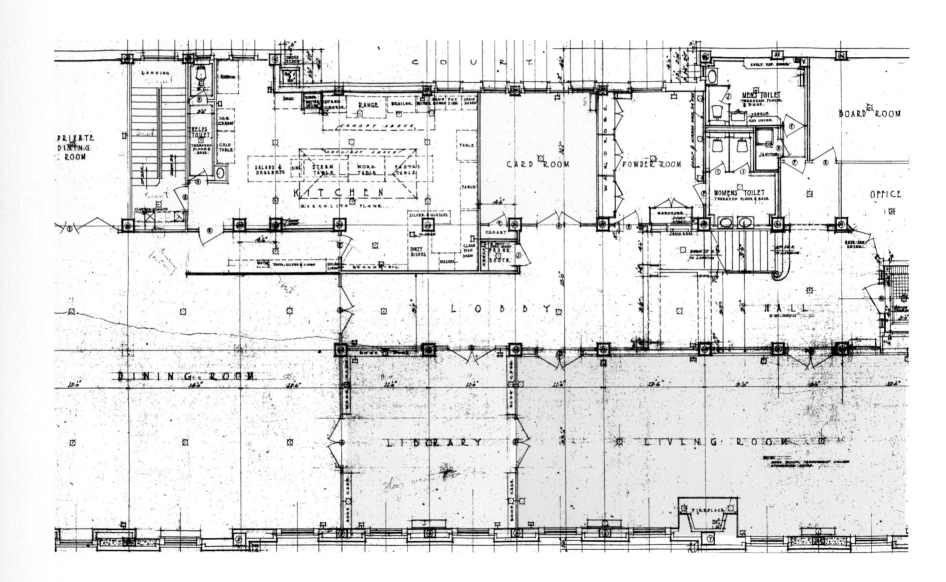

Chapter 5

Moving Forward ❧

THE WHIRLWIND OF POSTWAR REFURBISHMENT THAT BEGAN IN 1946 HAD largely been accomplished by 1950. Renovations and redecorations totaling more than $10,000 were accomplished in the summer of 1949 alone, including improvements to the kitchen and Ballroom. In 1950, the Club purchased new fireproof stage draperies, added storage under the stage, and finally resolved the problem of dampness in the Ballroom floor.

The Drawing Room was completely redecorated in 1951 with fireplace marble from Sweden, handsome louver doors, and wall-to-wall carpet. When announcing plans for the renovation, the House Trustee assured members that the new Drawing Room would be "elegant and in perfect taste."

The cultural and social activities offered by the Club enticed an increasing number of women to enter its doors. It was *the* club to join, *the* place to be in Seattle. Total membership reached 1,114 in the spring of 1950 with a long waiting list of applicants. Not only was the Club heavily booked for all kinds of activities, so many people were involved that it became more difficult to provide alternative meeting space in members' homes. The Summer Tea, which had once been held in the homes of one or two members, now took place in eleven different locations. When the Club was invited to make a contribution to the time capsule buried on Alki Point in celebration of the centennial of the 1851 Denny Party landing, it was not surprising that it offered the directory listing all of its members.

Postwar prosperity posed other challenges at the Club. Serving cocktails was the new fashion in entertaining. In September 1950, the board considered whether the Club should sponsor cocktail parties, but decided to reaffirm its long-standing policy of not serving liquor. As members who owned cars vied for parking spaces, the parking problem in front of the building became a source of constant frustration and aggravation.

Leisure pursuits were changing as well. Once the war ended, Club members and their husbands began to travel. Returning with colored slides of their trips instead of black-and-white snapshots, they presented travelogues to members eager to share vicariously in their journeys. Canasta was as popular as bridge. The monthly Book Discussion, which operated like a traditional book club within the Club's walls, quickly became a favorite new class, while square dance instruction delighted many members looking for lively activity.

Extraordinary speakers continued to be featured at the Club, some presenting social or political topics that might not have been considered in earlier years. In January 1951, a Speaker's Luncheon featured Miriam Van Waters, an advocate for prison reform, who had served for many years as the superintendent of the Massachusetts Reformatory

Presidents ❧	
Clara Smith	1950–51
Evelyn Gunther	1951–52
Margaret Ghormley	1952–53
Blanche Harris	1953–54
Marion Rogers	1954–55
Adelle Maxwell	1955–56
Margaret Grant	1956–57
Katherine Ashley	1957–58
Frances Morrill	1958–59
Ruth Sullivan	1959–60

🐉 In the News

June 25, 1950	Korean War begins
August 11, 1950	King County holds the first Seafair summer celebration
February 15, 1952	Museum of History and Industry opens
June 2, 1953	Queen Elizabeth II is crowned
July 27, 1953	Korean War ends
January 28, 1954	Dick's Drive-In opens in Wallingford
September 1, 1957	Elvis Presley performs at Sick's Stadium in Seattle
November 4, 1958	Catherine May becomes the first woman to represent Washington in Congress

The Summer Teas became so popular that in 1950, bridge was played in eleven homes in Broadmoor, and tea was served in the gardens of the Will Paddock home.

for Women in Framingham. Other speakers early in the decade included Senator Henry M. Jackson lecturing on "The Hydrogen Bomb: What Now?"; Dr. Dixy Lee Ray examining environmental issues with her review of *The Silent World* by Jacques Cousteau; and Senator Robert A. Taft of Ohio, who was seeking the 1952 Republican presidential nomination.

The holidays were as festive and celebratory as always. Fruitcakes and plum puddings made by the Club's kitchen were on sale for holiday entertaining and as Christmas gifts. There was a children's puppet show and the traditional New Year's Day Open House, but the Christmas dinner dance was informal due to a continuing dispute over the Club's nonunion work force; the musicians' union would not provide a band.

Just as in the country at large, movie stars were always a big attraction. Celebrity Luncheons featured a stellar lineup: Audrey Hepburn and the entire cast of *Gigi*, then playing at the Metropolitan Theatre; Jessica Tandy and Hume Cronyn; Alexis Smith and husband Craig Stevens; and actor Edward Everett Horton. In a different realm, the celebrated chef and food writer James Beard presented "Patio Cooking and the Spices of Life."

More members meant more interests and, inevitably, more classes. The board had already converted several bedrooms into classrooms as well as spaces for board and committee meetings. Following receipt of a bequest from the late Margaret Lyle, Club president in 1935, an east-facing room was redecorated, named the Lyle Room in her honor, and made available for use by all members. Mrs. Lyle had earned the special gratitude of the Club when she spearheaded the refinancing of the second mortgage during the 1930s.

By 1954, "to drink or not to drink" was an issue that would not go away. Members expected cocktail service, at least at special evening functions. The board investigated an annual liquor license but, because of the cost, decided instead to obtain a one-time banquet license for each event. Soon after, in another example of "keeping up with the times," a vending machine offering four brands of cigarettes was installed in the downstairs hall.

Family Tree Luncheon

Lotta Clark sponsored the first Mother-Daughter Luncheon at the Women's University Club in 1926. The event was a great success and became an annual Club tradition. In 1931, under the presidency of Frances MacBride, Allison Wanamaker suggested the event be expanded to include sisters, grandmothers, and other female relatives, and its name was changed to the Family Tree Luncheon. Held each year in August, the luncheon became a tradition at the Club. Mrs. MacBride's hobby was growing tuberous begonias at her home near Woodinville, and each year she donated hundreds of flowers, enough beautiful blooms to decorate the Club and provide corsages for the participants. These spectacular blossoms became the star attraction of the luncheons.

The *Seattle Post-Intelligencer* society editor devoted her August 26, 1954 column to a detailed description of the fashionable outfits worn by some of the luncheon participants, such as a mother "in a beige suit with black velvet toque [and] daughter in a gray sharkskin dress styled with Mandarin neckline and set-off by exotic dangling pearl earrings and a tiny black forward beanie. . . ." Members and their guests were entertained by speakers or by musical performances, sometimes given by members themselves.

By 1962 the Club boasted over seventy-five pairs of mother-daughter members, and in some cases these were three-generation families. Members were encouraged to invite their non-member relatives to the luncheons as well. Family Tree Luncheons continued into the 1970s, and Mrs. MacBride donated her favorite begonias until her home was sold. It is now the site of the Chateau Ste. Michelle winery.

Decorations for the Family Tree Luncheons always included masses of begonias donated by Frances MacBride. She is pictured here at her home near Woodinville.

▶ THE LONG WINDOWBOX of hanging bas-et-type tuberous begonias make a flaming blaze f color across the Philip D. Macbrides' interest-ng house near Woodinville. Mrs. Macbride is ictured standing in a planting of her hobby—flowers, their colors highlighted by a rhododen-dron background. She will bring more than 300 blossoms to the Women's University Club Family Tree luncheon on Tuesday, an annual custom.
—(Post-Intelligencer Photo by John M. "Hack" Miller.)

An eighteenth-century Japanese screen was given to the Club in 1952 by Marion Mesdag (née Blethen) in honor of her cousin, Club resident Elizabeth Hammons. The pines and cranes depicted on the six-fold screen are symbols of long life and strength in the face of adversity and are interpreted in Japan to be "happy" subjects. The artist is unknown.

Agnes Smith gave a slide presentation of her automobile tour of Europe at the Club in 1950.

With space at such a premium, the board began looking for a way to expand the Club's facilities. They were initially deterred by the unknown impact of plans to construct an interstate highway just across Sixth Avenue, about a block from the Club. As plans progressed, however, it became clear that Sixth Avenue would remain a major thoroughfare and that the highway might even prove beneficial for easier access to the Club.

It was evident that investing in much-needed parking for the short term and possible expansion in the long term would be a prudent decision. In 1954, the Club purchased the lot north of its building. Rental income from the newly-created parking lot quickly yielded a good return on the Club's investment. In 1956, the Club began to consider an expansion to resolve overcrowding in the dining room, as well as inadequacies in the kitchen and other facilities.

Growth of Seattle had its impact on Club operations, too. At the 1955 Annual Meeting, the corresponding secretary reported that 275 changes had been made in the *Yearbook*, many due to the various rural telephone exchanges that joined the Seattle dial system. This happened several times during the 1950s—with both telephone numbers and postal codes—giving the corresponding secretary much to do.

> *"During her trip to Europe last summer, Club member Ruth Moore kept her camera busy. As a result, she returned with an outstanding selection of beautiful pictures. We have all been anxiously awaiting a chance to see them, and tonight is the time for this delightful, vicarious Tour of the European Continent. All Club members are invited."*
>
> Bulletin (March 1951)

A variety of talented and interesting personalities highlighted the Club's roster of programs in the late 1950s. Spanish ballet star Roberto Iglesias and some of his troupe made a colorful appearance at the Club, and ballerina Alexandra Danilova provided a behind-the-scenes glimpse of her early training at the Russian Theatrical School. Seattle mountaineer Jim Whittaker drew a huge audience. V. W. van Gogh, nephew and namesake of the painter, spoke about the 1959 van Gogh exhibit at the Seattle Art Museum. Mr. van Gogh owned the majority of the paintings and drawings in the show.

New programs catered to changing times and current interests. The 1956 Antiques, Hobby and Collectors' Show attracted 529 people over two days and became a regular occurrence. With children now watching late-afternoon TV on a regular basis, a back-to-school party was held featuring entertainment by local TV star Stan Boreson of *KING's Klubhouse*, along with his dog No-Mo-Shun.

In 1957, Ewen Dingwall, Civic Center director, spoke about plans for the proposed world's fair in Seattle. A tour of Boeing's Renton plant took members through a mock-up of the Boeing 707, the world's first passenger jet. In 1959, Mrs. Edgar Woolley, personnel supervisor for Boeing's engineering division, spoke on "Women in the Space Age," and Dr. Charles Odegaard, newly appointed president of the University of Washington, gave the first of many enlightening lectures on education.

The Club faced a wrenching decision in 1958–59. With apartments becoming increasingly popular for young college-educated women who were working before they married, many of the Club's houseguests had become long-term residents. Several had reached an age at which they could no longer live safely in a building with no elevator and limited maid service. There were concerns about falls, fire evacuation, and senility. In the late 1940s, the board had decided to limit the maximum age of residents to seventy years, but enforcement had been lax. Now the board found itself compelled to act. Residents over the age of seventy were requested to move out by the end of April 1959.

Bob Cram, Seattle artist and illustrator, spoke at the Club in January 1955. Here he is shown creating a sketch of an audience member, Mrs. Henry A. Pratt, as Mrs. Errol W. Rawson looks on.

Treasures from private collections were shown at the Club's Antiques, Hobby and Collectors' Show in November 1955.

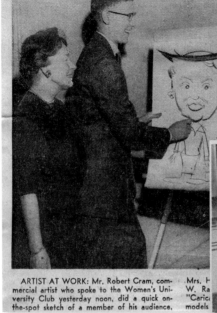

ARTIST AT WORK: Mr. Robert Cram, commercial artist who spoke to the Women's University Club yesterday noon, did a quick on-the-spot sketch of a member of his audience,

THURSDAY: Painting classes are held every Thursday in the Women's University Club. The instructor is Yvonne Humber (Mrs. Irving), standing, who is substituting for the regular teacher, Mrs. Angus Malloy, now traveling in Europe. Among those in the class are, from left, the Mesdames Jack A. Grant, John LeCocq, A. Winsor Johnson, Leslie Simkins (in rear) and Leon Bocker, all of whom were working with oils. A variety of arts and crafts classes are offered at the club. Sessions run from October through May.—Ron DeRosa, Times staff.

Painting has been one of the most popular and enduring classes at the Women's University Club. Pictured above are members in a 1957 class.

The board's letter to all residents regarding the issue said in part:

Unfortunately the ruling made some ten years ago on an age limit for Club residence was allowed to lapse and thus built up a false hope of no further age restriction. However the same problems have again risen and made it necessary for the present Board to reinstate an age limitation.

Our Committee has made a careful survey of the Club's facilities and services and finds the present set-up quite inadequate for the best welfare of the older residents.

With no elevator, limited maid service and strict City fire regulations to meet the Club finds itself unable to cope with the many problems that arise and the responsibility far too great for it to assume.

We particularly regret this for those of you to whom this has been home for many years and sincerely wish it were not necessary to uproot you at this time. This has been a very difficult decision to make and it saddens us to do so.

A Young Actives Group formed in the late 1950s to help young members, who often married and joined the Club right out of college, connect with each other and build their ties to the Club. They organized separate events for the group, such as a gala spring luncheon in May 1959 offering an opportunity to "put aside your mending and diapers, don your new spring bonnet and join us for a little frivolity." They staged a puppet show and gradually added more events for children. Eventually they were granted their own trustee and given responsibility for all children's programming at the Club.

By the time of the 1959 Annual Meeting, the residents affected by the age limit had departed and the board anticipated filling the vacant rooms by fall. The creation of a junior membership a year earlier (with half the entrance fee and half the monthly dues), expressly designed for women under the age of thirty-five, was bearing fruit, resulting in a more age-diverse membership.

Despite postwar renovations, the club was running out of space. As it catered to an expanding membership, the Club was becoming an increasingly interesting educational and cultural retreat. Members were focused on the future and the upcoming addition to their wonderful gathering place.

The Sportsmen's Symposium in September 1951 was planned to interest the husbands of members. Five speakers briefly discussed their sports specialty. Member Alice Jane Wanamaker, pictured at right, discussed foldboating, "a new water sport which is becoming very popular in this area."

The Seattle Times
Wednesday, Sept. 26, 1951

A FAVORITE PASTIME — FOLDBOATING: Miss Alice Wanamaker is among many who are finding foldboating a new and exciting sport. Photographed beside her foldboat in the garden of her Capitol Hill home, Miss Wanamaker is holding the double-bladed paddle used in propelling the canvas craft over swift running rivers. It is a tricky sport as the rower should be prepared for a dunking in the cold waters. As yet Miss Wanamaker hasn't capsized but she gives no promises for the future. In fact, her interest in the sport is so great she will speak on foldboating at the Women's University Club's Sportsman's Symposium tomorrow evening. Miss Wanamaker is a member of the Washington Foldboating Club. A foldboat is a canvas kayak for traveling rivers.

Stunt Night was one of the earliest traditions at the Women's University Club. Willye White is credited with originating these freewheeling members-only evenings, made up of skits, songs, and dances loosely based on a theme. The first Stunt Night took place in 1916.

Members were urged to arrange for child care, as this was a "girls' night out extravaganza." In 1941, Virginia Boren of the *Seattle Times* offered this advice to spouses in her March 2 column: "You'd better prepare to take care of the papooses and make your own grubstake, because the women members of the Women's University Club will NOT be 'Home on the Range.'" The theme that year was, naturally, "The Lazy U Ranch" and featured, among the other western-themed acts, a "Sally Rand Dude Ranch."

Members took all the parts, male and female, and inhibitions were cast aside. Political correctness was hardly the aim of these amateur thespians. They seemed to poke fun at popular figures of the times and at themselves. Even the formidable Dr. Mabel Seagrave, who had worked in a relief hospital abroad during World War I and was the principal overseer of the building of the new clubhouse in 1922, appeared regularly.

Other Stunt Night themes included "A Night in a London Music Hall" (1923), "Mother Goose Dinner" (1929), "A Night in Hawaii" (1938), and "Come as a Song" (1946). The 1942 show was a re-creation of the first Stunt Night, held in 1917 during World War I. Betty Cornelius attended as both a member and a reporter for the *Seattle Times*. Her story, which appeared on March 19, 1942, began, "Second song, same verse, a little louder, a little worse," and described the various skits and World War I costumed players. Her final paragraph was a tribute to the members of the Women's University Club:

> Riotous fun abounded for hours and everything was gayety, but few really forgot as they looked at overseas caps and wartime posters that there is work to be done. Everyone played and laughed their best and then, when all the fun was over, one could hear appointments being made for war work tomorrow. The women of the University Club played well—but they are also doing their work.

Margaret Evenson, who would become a Club president, remembered a Stunt Night when she dressed as a Zulu warrior, complete with necklaces of bones and teeth. She wore her costume home and scared her husband when he awoke from a sound sleep. She recalled that for the 1946 Stunt Night, held amid labor strife, a Club member dressed as a workman and carrying a lunchbox was accosted by workers who thought she was crossing a picket line.

The last Stunt Night was produced in 1950, but the memory of these wonderful productions will always be a part of the lore of the Women's University Club.

Stunt Night creativity was reflected in the clever programs.

Chapter 6

Bursting at the Seams ꝥ

B Y THE END OF THE 1950s, MORE SPACE WAS NEEDED TO ACCOMMODATE THE interests of the steadily growing roster of members. The Club had to expand, but in what direction? Recognizing that a growing number of families were moving to the suburbs, in late 1959 the Club polled members as to whether it should expand at the Sixth and Spring location or move out of the city. Members overwhelmingly supported the idea of adding to the existing facility.

Since the surface parking lot to the north of the clubhouse had always been considered a possible building site, the board voted unanimously in January 1960 to stay at Spring Street and authorized the Permanent Building Committee to hire an architect. In March, an architectural firm was retained to design the clubhouse renovation and addition on the parking lot property.

The architects proposed a three-phase plan. In the summer of 1960, the project would focus on remodeling existing rooms to make them more attractive and efficient, replacing old water lines, upgrading electrical systems to meet code, and installing new fire alarms. During this phase, the Board Room would be moved to the west end of the second floor and a new craft room created on the north side of that floor. In all, eleven rooms would be transformed for Club use.

The second phase, beginning in the fall of 1961, would involve constructing a new dining room with parking underneath and a completely new, expanded kitchen. The original dining room would be renamed the Gold Room and converted to multipurpose use. The third phase, for which no start date was set, would create a new foyer, a second entrance at the east end of the dining room, and substantial changes to the Ballroom. At the Semiannual Meeting in November

The rendering of the proposed 1962 addition to the Club, from the architectural firm of Durham, Anderson and Freed

1960, the board proposed to the membership a building assessment to pay for these renovations, which was overwhelmingly approved.

On July 18, 1962—during the summer of Century 21, the Seattle World's Fair—the Club held a dedication luncheon for the new addition. The dining room opened to rave reviews, and both the *Seattle Times* and the *Seattle Post-Intelligencer* featured large photo spreads publicizing the celebration. The "Century 21" edition of the Club cookbook, published to commemorate the opening, featured a cover illustration of the eighteenth-century Austrian porcelain stove that was a decorative highlight of the dining room's interior.

The Club took a break before proceeding with phase three of the remodel and revised the plan in order to add a second elevator. During this final phase, the Spring Street entrance to the Ballroom was closed, the lower-level windows covered, and a new stairway built to allow a gracious entry to the Ballroom from the Club interior and the new garage.

In May 1965, its work accomplished with much-heralded success, the Permanent Building Committee was disbanded.

Presidents ꝥ	
Isabel Pierce	*1960–61*
Eleanor Chapman	*1961–62*
Hope Keller	*1962–63*
Margaret Evenson	*1963–64*
Nikoline White	*1964–65*
Dorothy Lindsay	*1965–66*
Mary Martin	*1966–67*
Bertha Stone	*1967–68*
Amanda Merrick	*1968–69*
Millicent Martine	*1969–70*

In the News

March 26, 1960	New Seattle Central Library is dedicated
November 8, 1960	John F. Kennedy is elected president
April 21, 1962	Seattle World's Fair, Century 21, opens
October 12, 1962	Columbus Day windstorm, the most savage in West Coast history, damages 53,000 homes and kills 7 people in Washington and 35 in Oregon
November 22, 1963	President Kennedy is assassinated in Dallas
August 7, 1964	Gulf of Tonkin Resolution authorizes active combat role for U.S. troops in Southeast Asia
April 29, 1965	Magnitude-6.5 earthquake shakes western Washington
April 4, 1968	Rev. Martin Luther King Jr. is assassinated in Memphis
June 5, 1968	Senator Robert F. Kennedy is assassinated in Los Angeles
July 20, 1969	Apollo 11 astronaut Neil Armstrong walks on the moon

The focus on expansion did not interrupt the Club's exceptional curriculum. In April 1960, the Club honored Seattle artists George Tsutakawa, James H. FitzGerald, Glen Alps, Ray Jensen, and Paul Horiuchi at a special luncheon. Book Review, which had over 360 participants during these years, highlighted the country's two new states, Hawaii and Alaska, as well as the celebration of the Civil War centennial.

Speakers featured during this decade included Honor Earl—painter and daughter of Lord Maugham (chancellor of England in 1938) and niece of writer Somerset Maugham—who painted Noël Coward, the Queen Mother Elizabeth, and two of Churchill's grandchildren. Dr. John LeCocq, former chief of orthopedics at Children's Orthopedic Hospital, and his wife gave a presentation on their work in Indonesia with Project HOPE. Seattle gold medal rowers Ted Nash and Dan Ayrault and their coach Stanley Pocock shared their experiences at the Olympic Games in Rome. Mountaineer Jim Whittaker's presentation on his planned Mount Everest climb kicked off the speaker series in 1963, and he returned to the Club on October 27 after summiting; a capacity crowd turned out for both lectures.

The number of programs and classes increased, as did attendance, as membership reached 1,200. There were so many children's dance programs that the Dance Chairman became a member of the board for several years. The Family Tree Luncheon and the Autumn Brunch, the energetic "back to school" gathering where members signed up for the next year's activities, regularly sold out.

To publicize the heightened volume of activity, the monthly *Bulletin* doubled in size—from 3½ × 6 inches to 3½ × 8 inches—and increased from twelve pages to twenty-four. Feeding the volume of information about the Club's doings to Seattle newspapers' society page editors was a full-time job: the 1960–61 Publicity Trustee reported issuing 108 press releases, making the front page eight times, and getting twenty-six photos published.

Although members thought the new dining room was beautiful, they also believed it was noisy, and many considered the lighting to be too bright. In 1966, the Club removed the lighting fixtures and installed acoustical tile and new chandeliers. The refurbishment prompted comment from the women's page editor of the *Seattle Times* on September 26, 1966:

Our escort for dining out—he's the same one every time—is prone to enter most restaurants with the same question: "Is this a subversive meeting?" They're so dark that you could fool us as to what's in our plate—until the check comes. And the check, like the menu, has to be held close enough to the candle to scorch it before one can make out the figures.
The Women's University Club has always had light in its dining room, but not "pretty" light, with little ceiling spotlights. Now there are two great, beautiful chandeliers designed by Irene McGowan, and installed while Mrs. George Coleman Martin, [Club] President, was watching.

Eleanor Chapman, Mabel Chilberg, and Hope Keller posed with shovels big and small as Club members gathered on October 22, 1961, for the groundbreaking ceremony for the new addition to the Club.

Cookbook Treasures

The pages are slightly yellowed, the aroma a bit musty. Each page of the first cookbook, published in 1942, is carefully adorned with sketches of early Seattle drawn by a member of the Women's University Club. Fanciful drawings illustrate many recipes: Devil's Food Cake pictures a fiendish chef, and Egg Foo Yong sports two animated egg figures, while a top-hatted bumblebee adorns the Honey Cakes recipe.

Members share, in their own unique penmanship, 400 pages of their special recipes. Witty epigraphs grace the chapter title pages, ranging from Shakespeare's "My Salad Days—when I was Green in Judgment" to "Render to them their just Desserts" from the book of Psalms. The dark days of World War II are recalled in the second edition's suggestions for wartime cooking, containing substitutions for rationed items such as shortening and sugar.

Brimming with classic standbys that echo the time, the cookbook's offerings include Under the Sea Salad, Oyster Wiggle, and Tutti-Frutti Cake. The sometimes quaint ingredients include a 5-cent can of Hershey's chocolate, butter "the size of an egg," Karo syrup, and evaporated milk. Directions advise the cook to "bake in a moderate oven until done."

Later printings of *Treasured Recipes* celebrated the new dining room, in 1962, and the Club's Golden Anniversary, in 1964. The 1962 edition was illustrated and hand-printed by Jerralee Fernyhough.

A third cookbook was published in 1972. A few of the old recipes were kept, and many new ones added. Committee members did all of the hand-lettering of recipes. In 1988 a fourth version of the cookbook was created with new recipes and the addition of an index.

Each book mirrors its era, a tiny snippet of bygone times that linger in our memories, reminding us of the joys we have shared with friends and family around a dining room table.

1972

1988

We can live without Friends,
We can live without Books,
But civilized men
Cannot live without Cooks.

—Owen Meredith, *1942 WUC Cookbook*

"Did you know that there are only 47 more shopping days until Christmas? Well, here is a delightful and very practical gift for all of your friends and relatives who enjoy culinary arts—the Women's University Club Cook Book! We will gift wrap and mail as many copies as you wish anywhere in the USA, at no extra cost to you. Just leave your orders at the club office by December 10 and we'll do the rest."

Bulletin (November 1966)

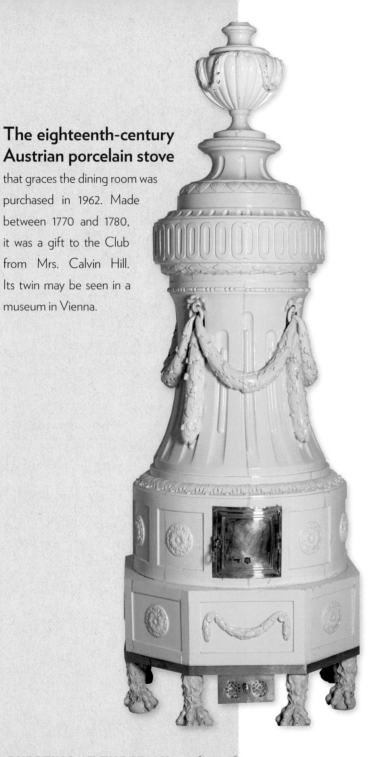

The eighteenth-century Austrian porcelain stove

that graces the dining room was purchased in 1962. Made between 1770 and 1780, it was a gift to the Club from Mrs. Calvin Hill. Its twin may be seen in a museum in Vienna.

Abundant newspaper coverage of the Club continued throughout most of the sixties, but changes in both quantity and content of publicity were coming. In excerpts from her 1968 Annual Report, the Publicity Trustee hinted at the future: "If all the clippings of Club news [from the newspapers] during the year were laid end-to-end on the ballroom floor, they would make a terrible clutter!" She stressed, however, "that the trend of the local women's sections of the daily newspapers is away from 'society news' and toward feature articles and news of general interest." She assured members of the Publicity Committee's "deep commitment to assuring the Club received its share of 'all the news that was fit to print.'"

In 1963, the gracefully aging Club kicked off a particularly newsworthy milestone—its fiftieth anniversary year. In November, the Club pulled out all the stops for its Golden Jubilee Black Tie Ball. A red carpet, rolled out by two costumed young men, greeted guests, who signed a parchment scroll with a quill pen. Dinner was served by candlelight, as in the Club's early years. Dessert featured cherries jubilee and a champagne toast followed by dancing. The birthday luncheon the following February included a stage presentation, *The Long Birthday Party*, written especially for the occasion.

Also in 1963, the Club joined a newly formed National Club Association, whose major objective was to reduce the 20 percent tax on private clubs, a remnant of the tax imposed during World War II on furs, jewelry, entertainment, and other luxuries. It had since been removed on all but dog and horse racing—and private clubs. In 1965, in a rare act of political activism, the corresponding secretary, at the request of the board, sent fifteen telegrams to congressmen and senators expressing the Club's position on the issue. Eventually the tax was repealed.

The restrictions of the $1 banquet license, which had to be purchased before each event and allowed cocktail service before but not during a meal, became a source of frequent complaints. For several years the board had balked at the $350 price tag of an annual liquor license plus additional costs for storage, waitstaff, and the like. In 1964, however, they directed the executive manager, Bernice McGarry, to evaluate the pros and cons of obtaining a liquor license. In August, the board held a special meeting with past presidents to discuss Mrs. McGarry's finding that benefits far outweighed costs. They concluded that cost and space issues could be resolved if members approved of the change. A ballot was mailed to 1,033 members and when the returns were counted, 797 had voted in favor of obtaining a Class H liquor license. With the license in hand, the Club installed a bar in the Gold Room that became a popular gathering place for pre-luncheon and before-dinner socializing. Members could henceforth enjoy alcoholic beverages whenever they dined, and it was not long before wine dinners became a popular dining room feature.

The Club did impose a few of its own restrictions, however. The *Bulletin's* December 1966 Club Notes reminded members: "No Drinking in the Club when teen dances are in session." And the board and committees occasionally opted to retain traditions of the past, as in August 1967 when they decided to forgo alcohol in the punch at the Summer Tea.

In the mid-1960s, cooking classes became an important part of Club offerings. In October 1964, Peter Canlis opened the International Cuisine series, an event featured on the society page. The *Seattle Times* reported on October 25:

> When Mr. Peter Canlis gave the first demonstration of international cookery . . . more than 100 women applauded as he told the secrets of poaching salmon and making mustard mayonnaise. . . . The women learned some of the tricks for successful tossed salads such as: Never tear the lettuce but cut it instead for crispness; add the croutons last, after the dressing, so they will be crisp; put all the heavy ingredients in the bottom of the bowl before tossing; make your bacon bits by cooking tiny squares of the bacon over a very slow fire until all the fat is completely melted.

The next year, the Music, Arts and Crafts Trustee announced an expanded Cuisine series whose instructors included Everett Boss, the

An International Cuisine presentation in 1964 featured Peter Canlis, shown here with his wife and Masao Nakishima demonstrating a tossed salad for the first lesson of the series.

"Monsieur Gourmet" columnist for the *Seattle Times;* the ladies of the Greek Orthodox Church of the Assumption, who taught a class on Greek pastry; a European-trained chef whose specialty was flaming desserts; and a chef from United Airlines. Cuisine classes were here to stay.

Book Review had its hand in the cooking scene, too. Maurine Kelley, 1965–67 Dining Room Trustee, reviewed *Mastering the Art of French Cooking* by Julia Child and her French colleagues, Simone Beck and Louisette Bertholle. In addition to discussing cookbooks in general—including the Club's own publication—Mrs. Kelley provided observations from her years as the "Prudence Penny" advice columnist for the *Seattle Post-Intelligencer.*

The sixties were a time of contentious debate about the role of women. As women began to obtain positions to which they formerly had little access, their successes were reflected at the Club's podium. In 1962, Marianne Means, the youngest reporter to cover the White House for Hearst Headline Service, spoke at a Celebrity Luncheon. Dr. Dixy Lee Ray, director of

Seattle's Pacific Science Center and later Washington's first female governor, spoke in 1964.

Like their predecessors during the suffragist era, the board refused to lend the Club's name to any public activity involving women's rights, but actively courted speakers on the subject. In 1963 the board declined to become a sponsor of a University of Washington conference on the role of women, but in 1965 invited Dr. Bernice Sachs, a leading physician at Group Health Cooperative, to speak on "Women's Destiny—Choice or Chance?"

The war in Vietnam was also a troubling issue during the 1960s—one on which Club members were as deeply divided as the broader community. The subject appeared in Club programs in many guises. In 1965, Senator Henry M. Jackson gave a Current Events program titled "In Pursuit of

National Security." KCTS-TV manager Loren B. Stone, returning from six months in Vietnam working for USAID, spoke on "How Television Came to Vietnam."

The 1966–67 International Speakers series began with a lecture by Agnes Newton Keith, a writer famed for her books about her life in Borneo before World War II and her subsequent internment, with her husband and son, in a Japanese prison camp there. Her talk—a look at the United States from an international point of view—was based on her book *Children of Allah*, written during her husband's nine-year tenure with a UN mission in Libya. Introducing the topic, the Club *Bulletin* took the opportunity for a rare—and passionate—political comment:

> *We in the United States are citizens of every race, color and creed; there is no single national image of us, other than that we are generally well-fed. We are heterogeneous in almost everything except our national passion for freedom, and we are frustrated in our search for freedom as men in other countries are frustrated in their search for bread. We love to be loved—but bombs, riches and worldly power don't make people love us.*

Drugs and the trouble on college campuses were also subjects of interest. The September 1966 *Bulletin* announced a program to be held on November 15: "The LSD . . . fad is causing a lot of commotion. If you want some sound information about the dreamy stuff, Dr. Gordon G. Bergy . . . director of Student Health Services at the University [of Washington] . . . will share his professional knowledge

On February 11, 1964, members enjoyed an original play, *The Long Birthday Party*, at the fiftieth birthday luncheon. Two members portrayed flappers of the 1920s.

Beverly Carey, Darlene Magnano, and Dorothy Bohlke demonstrate how guests at the Golden Jubilee ball would register when they attended the Club's gala fiftieth anniversary celebration.

with us." Programs in 1969 titled "Campus Unrest: Extent, Cause, Cure" and "Kids, Pot and Community: Solution or Chaos?" further explored these topics.

Not only were current events shaking things up, but the ground beneath Seattle was quivering, too. In April 1965 a major earthquake hit the city, causing considerable damage in many areas, including the clubhouse. Thirty-nine rooms required repair, at a total cost of $2 million.

Later in 1965, the City of Seattle approached the board about plans for improvements to the small triangular strip across the street from the Club building, on the corner of Sixth Avenue and Seneca Street between the sidewalk and the railing above the freeway. The city proposed to construct a fountain and install landscaping in the space and invited the Club to consider paying for the fountain. After consulting with its architect, who advised that the $8,000 quoted by the city was considerably less than the fountain was likely to cost, the board declined to make the gift. Architect Floyd Naramore stepped forward to donate the funds needed, and the fountain, designed by George Tsutakawa, was dedicated on June 13, 1967. In collaboration with the Central Association of Seattle, the Club hosted the artist and numerous city dignitaries at a luncheon to honor Mr. Naramore following the dedication.

Two months later, the board's minutes noted that "the committee for the summer tea on August 23 [has] chosen 'Three Coins in a Fountain' as its theme. (Page Mr. Naramore!) They hope to have a fountain as part of the dining room decor into which guests would throw simulated gold coins (and make a wish, we assume). The idea was received enthusiastically."

In 1966, the board began talking about the possibility of creating an endowment, the first major effort to systematically accumulate funds for future needs. President Mary Martin suggested that such a fund might include the current Memorial Fund, Birthday Fund, and other special categories. Members could donate to this fund in the form of memorials, birthday gifts for friends and family, or bequests. The new fund was introduced at the fifty-third Birthday Party, where it was generously accepted and supported.

Floyd Naramore, a Seattle architect, shown here with sculptor George Tsutakawa, donated $65,000 for a fountain to be built across the street from the Women's University Club. A drawing of the fountain, prepared by Mr. Tsutakawa, is also shown.

GEORGE TSUTAKAWA, left, and FLOYD A. NARAMORE
With a model of the plaza

Architect Donates $65,000 Plaza, Fountain to Seattle

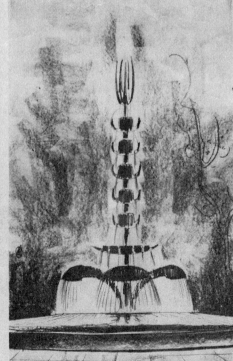

The following year, the board looked into a number of organizational issues, including several ideas about reallocating programs among trusteeships. Among the changes, activities that had been grouped under Entertainment were placed for the first time under the umbrella of a new Traditional Events Trustee.

The Policy Review Committee also examined the process for nominating, electing, and installing the new board each year. The March Posting Party—an annual staple of Club life in the early decades, during which nominees for president and the board were introduced to members before their names were posted on the bulletin board—had fallen by the wayside. Instead, the new president and trustees were announced at the Birthday Party in February. As the committee explained in its report,

The main problem, it seems, relates to the announcement of nominees as early as February, the election in March, and the period of over two months before the new President and Trustees actually take office. The committee felt that while a period of orientation is very important, the present schedule is a very confusing and trying one for all concerned. The weight of duties and responsibilities in the position of President is such that she begins to feel "in stride" only about the middle of her term, or the first of January, and this

Looking Back at the WUC Chorus

In 1937, several members asked Amy Worth if she would start and direct a choral group at the Club. For twenty-six years, the history of the chorus and the musicality of Mrs. Worth were inseparable.

A noted composer and publisher, this shy but joyous lady wrote songs that were recorded and sung by such eminent singers as Lotte Lehmann, Kirsten Flagstad, Richard Tucker, and Jeanette MacDonald. Mrs. Worth composed art songs, cantatas, and hymns—many specifically for the chorus. Mrs. Worth was made an honorary life member of the Club in recognition of her many contributions.

Chorus programs often included chamber music, sometimes featuring solos by Club members, many of whom were professional musicians working as music teachers and as performers. In the late 1960s the chorus became an integral part of the Christmas Teas.

After Amy Worth retired, Leone Turner—a member of the chorus, a soloist, and a choral director in her own right—directed the chorus for fifteen years. There followed a series of directors, both men and women, including past Club president Cynthia Hamp and members Marianne Wiebe and Delores Fox. Anne Questad, longtime Club member, was the group's accompanist for many years. Prominent Seattle composer/directors Carol Sams and George Shangrow also led the chorus, as did Ann Erickson.

For many years the chorus performed in the spring as well as at Christmas, singing Mrs. Worth's Easter music as spring art songs. In addition, individual members of the group have been asked to add musical luster to other Club functions such as the Posting Party and other traditional events. They have also been strolling minstrels for the Spring Arts Fair.

The musical education acquired by members of the chorus throughout its long history has been appreciated by all of those who have passed through its ranks. The camaraderie that has ensued has built the closest of bonds. And the ability to give pleasure to Club audiences has filled every chorus member's heart with joy.

feeling is almost immediately changed with the announcement of the new President. The committee was unanimous in feeling that this greatly complicates a President's and a Board's sense of direction. There is, too, the fact that many members, not fully informed or aware of Club details, assume that the President-elect is, in fact, already in office, and the President, hardly half way through her year, is already being thanked for the job she has done.

The committee recommended that the announcement of the slate of nominees for board positions be moved to the third Wednesday in February, with the election the third Wednesday in April, and that newspaper publicity coincide with the Annual Meeting in May. The members heartily endorsed the changes and made the Policy Review Committee a permanent feature of Club governance.

In September 1968, *Seattle* magazine published a hard-hitting article scornfully attacking most of the private clubs in the city. The author appeared to be atypically kind to the Women's University Club, however, criticizing only the use of italicized words in the monthly *Bulletin* and the busy schedule offered to members, noting that "it would be hard to imagine any club providing a more exhausting round of events. . . . Classes and lectures begin at 9 A.M. and run far into the night."

Italics criticisms aside, the comments regarding the overflowing schedule were certainly *true*. The interests of members were many and varied, and the board made a sincere effort to respond to their changing needs and wishes. Mainstream and Goodevening lectures, Cuisine classes, Handy Hannah, and a Philosophy class were among the diverse activities created in response to specific ideas and suggestions derived from the committees' program planning sessions.

To the pleasure of everyone, long-standing traditions held their own amid the burgeoning agenda of new activities. The Christmas Tea and Musicale, as well as the Twelfth Night celebration, had to be expanded to two days in order to accommodate all who wished to attend. Members' strong affinity for the performing arts inspired groups to organize to attend symphony concerts, operas, and traveling Broadway shows. The Club offered dinner before the performances and provided buses to take members to the theater. Trips to noted gardens and spots of historical interest reflected members' curiosity and interest in travel, as did the slide shows they presented on their exotic adventures: Morocco; Moscow and Leningrad; Scandinavia; East Africa from Addis Ababa to Zanzibar; the mountains of Iran; and the Himalayas and Karakoram Range, where an intrepid member hired a guide and drove to the 5,000-foot level of Hunza Peak.

The sixties were a tumultuous decade of war, inflation, financial stresses, building construction, and an earthquake, but the Club weathered it well. In November 1968 the treasurer asserted, "The Women's University Club has a reputation in this city for giving its members the most for the least, and we will continue this policy and make our club 'the hostess with the mostest for the leastest.'" The dining room received accolades from all who entered, and now featured the added attraction of cocktails. Decorum was tested as fashions transitioned from skirts to pantsuits. Across the street, the Naramore Fountain splashed in Freeway Park. The bylaws and rules had undergone revisions that set the course for the future. The decade that began with bouffant hairdos and pillbox hats ended with "You've come a long way, baby."

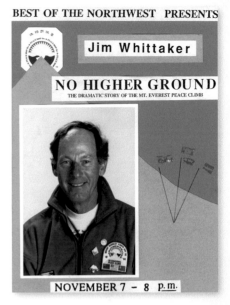

BEST OF THE NORTHWEST PRESENTS

Jim Whittaker

NO HIGHER GROUND
THE DRAMATIC STORY OF THE MT. EVEREST PEACE CLIMB

NOVEMBER 7 – 8 p.m.

Jim Whittaker, noted mountaineer, was always a popular speaker.

ATTENTION: CLUB MEMBERS

At present we have guest rooms available for occupancy, both on a permanent basis and for the interval of the World's Fair. We hope, through our membership, to have all rooms rented for Century 21. Rental rates for transients will be $7.00 per day including breakfast, with lunch and dinner available on an ala carte basis. This would be an ideal location for out-of-town visitors. We would like to take care of your guests and other recommended guests.

Reservations are being made now with our Club Manager, Mrs. McGarry.

A notice in the *Bulletin* advertised guest rooms available for out-of-town visitors during Seattle's Century 21 Exposition in 1962. Rental rates were $7 per day and included breakfast. Other meals were available on an à la carte basis.

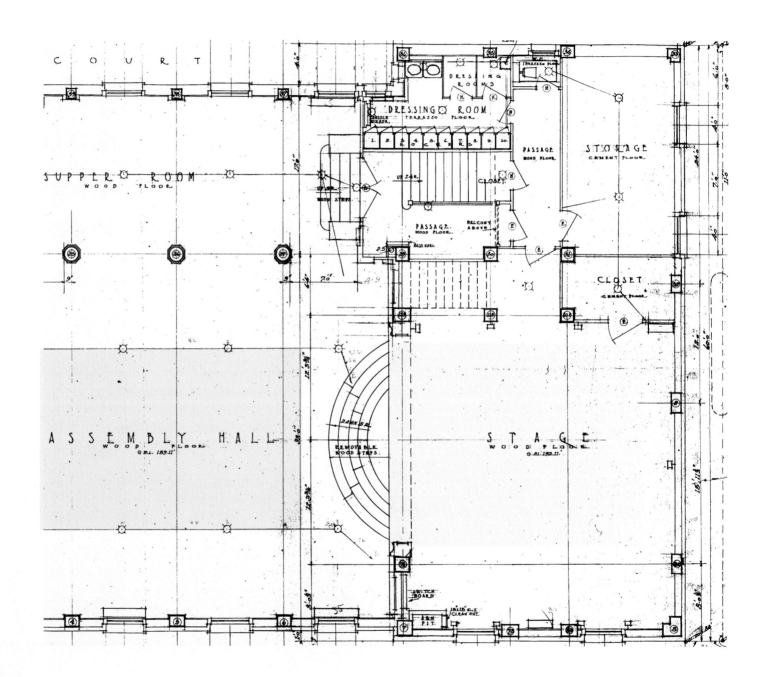

Chapter 7

Changing Times ❦

IXTY YEARS HAD PASSED SINCE THE FOUNDERS CREATED THE WOMEN'S University Club. Like their predecessors, members in the 1970s were well-educated and accomplished women who were involved in the community, while many more were in the workforce. Membership was fully subscribed, with over 200 on the waiting list. To keep prospective members in touch with the Club through what was sometimes a wait of two years or more,

the Club held a series of "Ladies in Waiting" coffees. In 1974 the resident membership was raised to 1,500, and by the end of the decade this new maximum was reached. At the same time, to address concerns about the dwindling number of junior members, special efforts were undertaken to create programs and activities that would attract this age group.

Times had changed in ways the Club's founders could not have imagined. By 1970, only thirteen residents remained; in August, the board voted to phase out the residential program entirely and permit no new overnight guests of any kind. The last resident left the Club in 1974.

The high rate of inflation that had begun in the 1960s, combined with the declining number of residents, challenged the Club's finances, particularly in the dining room. The board and executive manager debated whether to resolve the problem of losses by cutting staff or wages, raising dining room prices, or raising dues. When the problem persisted into the new decade, the board sponsored a series of special dinner parties to generate additional member usage: a St. Patrick's Day dinner, a crab and beer feed, a hillbilly party, and a Scandinavian smorgasbord. A Mother's Day dinner, scheduled for the first time in May 1971, proved to be a successful innovation. Such measures failed to reverse the dining room's losses, however.

Early in 1971, the Club received a letter from the IRS warning that its outside income exceeded the permitted percentage of its total revenue. With the Club's tax-exempt status at stake, the board and executive manager immediately took steps to reduce the amount of outside income, which was another blow to the bottom line. The board polled members in September 1972, offering three options: raise dues, raise prices, or set a monthly dining room minimum of $3.50 in the form of scrip issued to each member. Seventy-two percent favored the dining room minimum, although some members expressed concerns that scrip could be lost or might look like food stamps. Based on the latter concern, the board decided to handle the scrip as a bookkeeping item and authorized the addition of the charge. The move promptly swamped the accounting department; the following February, the board agreed to purchase an addressograph and a billing machine to handle the extra work.

Committee chairmen in charge of lectures and classes had no end of hot topics from which to choose in the early 1970s, whether from a

Presidents ❦	
Imogene Rogan	*1970–71*
Jeannette Acker	*1971–72*
Berniece Matthews	*1972–73*
Jean LeGros	*1973–74*
Frances Heaverlo	*1974–75*
Dorothy Lynch	*1975–76*
Doris Coulter	*1976–77*
Louise Schnatterly	*1977–78*
Roberta Moore	*1978–79*
Virginia Woodruff	*1979–80*

April 1971	Starbucks Coffee Company opens its first store, in Pike Place Market
April 16, 1971	Billboard reading "Will the last person leaving Seattle—turn out the lights" appears near Sea-Tac Airport in reaction to local economic downturn
November 2, 1971	Seattle voters approve initiative to preserve Pike Place Market
November 24, 1971	D. B. Cooper parachutes from a skyjacked 727 with $200,000 ransom
April 29, 1974	Construction of the Trans-Alaska Pipeline begins
April 4, 1975	Bill Gates and Paul Allen start Micro-Soft (the hyphen was removed in 1976); move to Bellevue in 1978
April 30, 1975	The fall of Saigon marks the end of the Vietnam War
July 1975	Seattle Opera stages Richard Wagner's *Der Ring des Nibelungen* for the first time
June 1, 1979	Seattle SuperSonics win the NBA World Championship

political, social, or cultural perspective. Dr. Giovanni Costigan, a favorite liberal professor at the University of Washington, gave three lectures on "Patterns of Revolution" in 1971. A faculty member who spoke on racism and ethnic conflict was so controversial that a Club member wrote to the board to congratulate them on having the courage to invite him to speak.

Women's issues were much in the national news and on the minds of members. The 1971 Book Discussion class selected as its theme "Modern Women as Serious Writers: Books That Speak to the Condition of Women in Our Time." Books on the list included *To the Lighthouse* by Virginia Woolf, *Not for Publication* by Nadine Gordimer, *The Mandarins* by Simone de Beauvoir, *The Prime of Miss Jean Brodie* by Muriel Spark, and *I Know Why the Caged Bird Sings* by Maya Angelou. The Club's attorney, Muriel Mawer, gave a talk on "Women's Legal Rights." In 1972, when the Club scheduled a speaker on the sexual revolution, the Publicity Trustee reported to the board that the newspapers, which had declined to cover the Summer Teas that year, were keenly interested in reporting on the lecture.

Program subjects ranged from the mundane to the sublime. In 1972, Interior Design scheduled a lecture and demonstration titled "From Antiques to Plastics," and Peter Hallock, music director at St. Mark's Cathedral, presented a program on changes in sacred music.

Clothing styles and fabrics were evolving. Women wearing trousers in public places and particularly within the clubhouse sparked many interesting conversations about dress codes. These discussions may even have inspired the "History of Pants" program at the Club's 1970 Family Tree Luncheon. Well-known Seattle fashion retailer John Doyle Bishop staged the first fall fashion show and luncheon with such great success that it prompted evening fashion events featuring men's clothing as well. Classes in sewing with Stretch and Sew polyester and Ultrasuede fabrics were added following their introduction in stores.

In 1972, the board approved a new program called President's Choice, which permitted each president to sponsor one or more programs each year. The Club also expanded the current affairs program by instituting Mainstream, an afternoon lecture series. Among the outstanding individuals brought by the series were actresses Celeste Holm and Olivia de Havilland, Pulitzer Prize–winning director Josh Logan, singer Patrice Munsel, journalists Harrison Salisbury and Virginia Graham, and TV personalities Kitty Carlisle and Peter Lind Hayes.

Local figures were often on the calendar as well. Jean Enersen, the first anchorwoman on local television news, appeared at a Club luncheon. King County Councilwoman Bernice Stern, a good cook as well as an accomplished politician, presented a Cuisine class on hors d'oeuvres. Barbara Coffin, a Roosevelt High School grad, opera singer turned cabaret performer at Rosellini's 410 restaurant,

> *Mrs. James Hyde, Speakers Trustee, presented her report to the Annual Meeting in rhyme. The poem concluded:*
>   *"We had 26 programs, you see,*
>   *And 1588 people attended.*
>   *Thank you for letting me be your trustee,*
>   *I'm almost sorry the year has ended."*
>
> Annual Meeting Minutes (5/27/70)

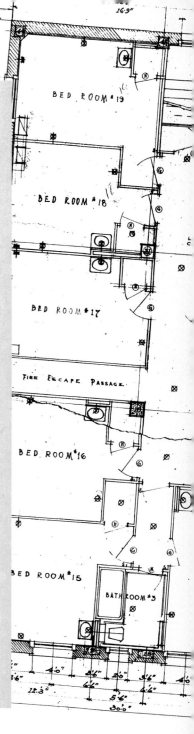

Houseguests

Bedrooms on the second and third floors were rented to individuals referred to as houseguests by the Club. Bathrooms were down the hall and the water pressure was low, noted Frances Owen, a houseguest from 1924 to 1929, but the food was "excellent." Jean Saunders's tiny room on the third floor in the back of the building cost $91 per month when she moved to the Club in 1938. All the rooms were "small but very sweet and comfortable," said Anne Neal, a guest in the 1950s. When Pat Bowman became a guest in 1965, "the rent for the smallest room was $135 which included linens, laundry, mail and phone service, and two meals a day, plus sandwiches for lunch." Joan Poliak, a guest from 1952 to 1956, said, "The housekeeping was marvelous—they made my bed, vacuumed and even picked up my clothes. I didn't have to do anything. I had never had it so good!"

Romance was always in the air. In 1958, Jane Gerhardt's room was over the front entrance, from which she could see the College Club. She and the other young residents liked to check out the comings and goings across the street. Fresh out of college, Jean Saunders met her future husband, Ben, on a blind date arranged by a College Club friend. As the romance progressed, she and Ben played badminton in the Ballroom, where suction cups held the net to the walls. Men were forbidden above the first floor; Ben proposed to Jean in the Library. Edith Swanson, who lived at the Club in 1959–60, tells of a "gentleman" who left his hat on the stair banister as a Do Not Disturb sign indicating that he and his lady friend wanted privacy in the room set aside for entertaining guests.

The houseguests appreciated the caring staff at the Club and the safety of the location. Anne Neal, a night nurse at Virginia Mason Hospital, felt quite safe walking back to the Club after work at 11:00 P.M. Residents loved the gracious atmosphere, the outstanding food, and the friendships they developed, many of which lasted a lifetime. The young houseguests enjoyed interacting with the older residents, who offered advice such as that recorded by Pat Bowman: "Girls, when you walk down the street, look up at the sky, not down. You will then see Mount Rainier instead of the spit on the sidewalk."

Sharon Jepperson was a houseguest in 1962 while she was an IBM trainee. At dinnertime she and the other trainees became acquainted with several residents and developed the art of making polite conversation. During her weeks at the Club she realized that "[w]omen were a force to be reckoned with," and said this awareness provided her with the confidence that helped her succeed in her career with IBM and later as a wife and mother.

In 1973, the guest rooms were closed, but Doris Wilk, who had moved to the Club in 1957, was allowed to stay on until she could make her planned move to Pasco, Washington. The building was locked at 11:00 P.M. Although Doris was alone in the big dark building until 7:00 A.M., she wasn't lonely. In every corner, on every step, were happy memories of all the friends she had made in her fifteen years as a resident. They were very good company.

Goya Print

This original reproduction of a painting by Spanish artist Francisco Goya (1746–1828) was created by a process known as soft-ground etching. Black ink was pressed onto white paper, then hand-painted with watercolors to produce the original prints. The artwork was a gift to the Club by Willye White in the 1970s.

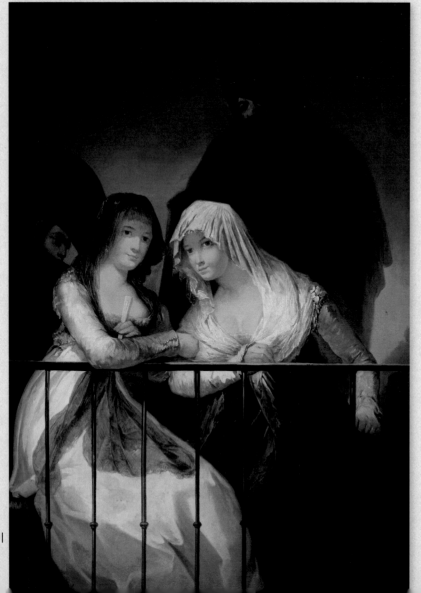

and the "fat lady" for the Sonics, performed at a Supper Club evening. Well-known Seattle photographer Josef Scaylea and *Skid Road* author Murray Morgan gave talks with a Northwest theme. University of Washington professor Pepper Schwartz spoke on "Marriage and the Family in the 1970s."

One addition to Club programming resulted from a bequest from member Carrie B. Raser, who died in 1977. Her gift was used for many years to sponsor annual lectures, including one in 1979 featuring Malcolm Miller, renowned expert on Chartres Cathedral. Another innovation was a classic film series. Audiences of over 150 regularly attended movies from Hollywood's golden years such as *Laura, Camille, Citizen Kane, Meet Me in St. Louis, The Philadelphia Story,* and *Mister Roberts.*

Of course, not all innovations worked perfectly. In 1978, the Juniors/Youth Trustee reported to the board on the unhappy incidents of that year's Halloween Party "as abetted by the offspring attending and the magician, who added unexpected horrors. On the positive side, it was the largest Halloween Party since 1974 with 109 adults and 96 children (from 2 to 12, average age 5) for a total of 205. It only seemed like more. . . ."

Many Club members were avid travelers. During the seventies, opportunities for members to travel together on Club-sponsored adventures were greatly expanded. In 1974, a trip to Ashland, Oregon, was organized, preceded by two lectures by Virginia Dearborn, head of Ballard High School's English department. She had taught Shakespeare at the Club for many years but had only recently become a member. The Ashland trip became a regular summer feature.

Interior Design sponsored trips to the home of Senator and Mrs. Henry Jackson and the Governor's Mansion in Olympia. A trip to Port Townsend featured tours of Victorian homes. Within King County, trips ranged from a walking tour of Freeway Park to a tour and lunch at Chateau Ste. Michelle winery.

The fifty-year-old building was showing signs of age as various systems began to fail. The main storm drain under the Club rotted out, and leaks in the Gold Room and the ladies' lavatory next to the Ballroom caused considerable damage. The elevator developed problems, the hot water storage tank in the boiler room had to be replaced, and the heating system and roof also required major repairs.

In the midst of repairs to the old, the board also made way for the new, authorizing in February 1973 the purchase of a microwave oven from Seattle City Light for $300; a demonstration of how it worked was included in the cost. The purchase of mimeograph and stencil-cutting equipment permitted in-house printing of all enclosures, flyers, programs, posters, and menus in "two busy rooms on the third floor."

Throughout these years, the Club continued to invest in the elegant rooms that gave members such pleasure. Four small rooms on the second floor were combined in 1971 and became known as the Spring Room. In 1977, a gift from Margretta Hillman permitted the Club to combine three rooms into a large gathering space appropriately titled the Hillman Room. As renovations proceeded, items that were no longer needed were sold or given away. In 1978, the House Trustee reported to the board, "The Salvation Army has been gifted with the unsaleable, unsalvageable and unloved."

The Club hosted a Frederick & Nelson International Fashion Show in February 1976. Couture designs from Paris, London, and many other cities were among the 150 pieces of apparel modeled at the show.

Books Reviewed in 1972–73 included: Eleanor and Franklin *by J. Lash;* The Terminal Man *by M. Crichton;* Captains and Kings *by T. Caldwell;* George S. Kaufman *by H. Teichmann; and* Mary Todd Lincoln: Her Life and Letters *by J.G. Turner.*

Board Meeting Minutes (8/14/72)

Sentimental journey to 60

At the sixtieth birthday luncheon in 1974, sixty-year members were honored. Pictured are Elizabeth Dickerson, Blanche Wenner, and Edna Vaupell. On the right is Jean LeGros, the president that year.

The Club also added substantially to its collection of antique furniture, including a George III bookcase-on-chest and an English wine table. Generous bequests also increased the Club's collection of art treasures. In 1977, a bequest from Mildred M. Miller permitted the purchase of the stone sculpture *Preening Merganser* by local artist Tony Angell. The number of gifts and bequests prompted the Club, at the 1978 Annual Meeting, to create the Memorial and Gift Committee to review all proposed gifts and make recommendations to the board as to their acceptance.

In a world of rapidly changing mores, proper etiquette, attire, and decorum required constant attention. A new waitress who was doing an excellent job otherwise was advised to improve her hairstyle, and the board reluctantly approved pants as acceptable attire for female staff. The Membership Trustee offered each member the choice of being listed in the Directory by her husband's name, as had been the tradition since the Club's founding, or by her first name; on a similar topic, the board decided that "Mrs." would remain the proper form for staff to use when addressing members.

Although the Club's leaders were notoriously frugal, the board still considered mentioning money to be rude, declaring that "prices [may] not . . . be included in posters" put up to advertise Club events, and continuing to resist the urgings of the painting class to put prices on artworks for sale by Club members. Other stories of Yankee thrift from this decade include one about an indignant member who wrote to the board, on her return home from a Club field trip, citing the inappropriateness of the bus driver asking those over sixty-five to raise their hands. If this was for the purpose of ascertaining the correct ferry fare, she

The Music, Arts and Crafts Trustee reported to the Board that "45 attended the latest Interior Design Class which was excellent in spite of the fact that [the speaker] talked on walls so long he didn't get to windows."

Board Meeting Minutes (2/12/73)

Preening Merganser, sculpted in stone by the artist Tony Angell, was purchased with a bequest from Mildred M. Miller. It was presented to the Club at a special luncheon featuring Mr. Angell in May 1977. Mr. Angell is a well-known artist, author, environmentalist, and bird-watcher.

wanted to know, who got the savings? The board was unfazed, however, when the 1976 Twelfth Night speaker requested a bottle of good scotch instead of an honorarium; they readily agreed.

In 1976, the Club received a proposal by a developer interested in the vacant lot to the north of the Club's property. A building next door was a certainty, he said—probably a hotel, with excavations going down three stories. He proposed doing excavation work under the Club building also, which would give the Club more parking, and offered to purchase air rights over the Club.

The board was inclined to protest the development. In the end, however, Club representatives met with the hotel's developer. One of the board's major concerns was that digging the hotel foundation much deeper than the Club's lower level would cause slippage because of the springs known to be in the hillside. The parties agreed to perform a structural survey of the Club's property to alleviate these concerns. An agreement was also reached to provide the Club access to the hotel garage for evening events.

American society changed in the 1970s, as did the Women's University Club. The recession early in the decade—Seattle's now-famous Boeing Bust—strained the Club's finances for a time, but could not diminish the enthusiasm for challenging classes and fresh ideas. Formality lost ground in the dress code, reflecting modern women's preference for pantsuits and other more casual attire as well as acceptance of the increasing independence of single working women. The Club's residential hotel for women closed after fifty years in operation.

What stayed constant, however, was the gracious ambience of the Club with its beautifully decorated interiors. While continuing to grow and adapt to the world around it, the Club retained its timeless presence as a quiet oasis of friendship and elegance.

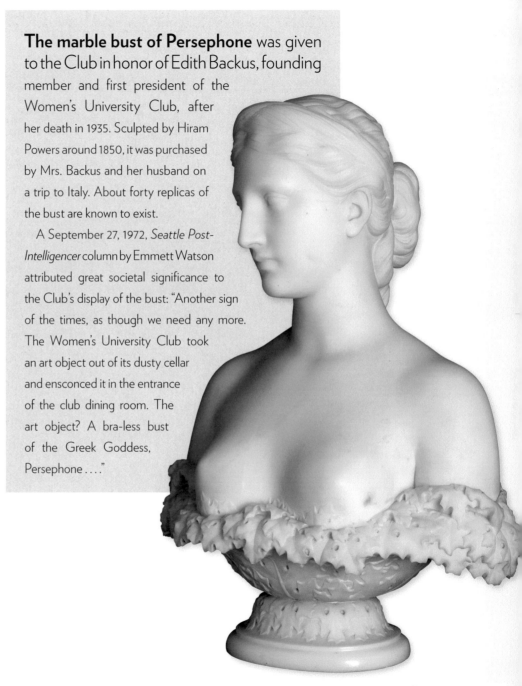

The marble bust of Persephone was given to the Club in honor of Edith Backus, founding member and first president of the Women's University Club, after her death in 1935. Sculpted by Hiram Powers around 1850, it was purchased by Mrs. Backus and her husband on a trip to Italy. About forty replicas of the bust are known to exist.

A September 27, 1972, *Seattle Post-Intelligencer* column by Emmett Watson attributed great societal significance to the Club's display of the bust: "Another sign of the times, as though we need any more. The Women's University Club took an art object out of its dusty cellar and ensconced it in the entrance of the club dining room. The art object? A bra-less bust of the Greek Goddess, Persephone . . . ."

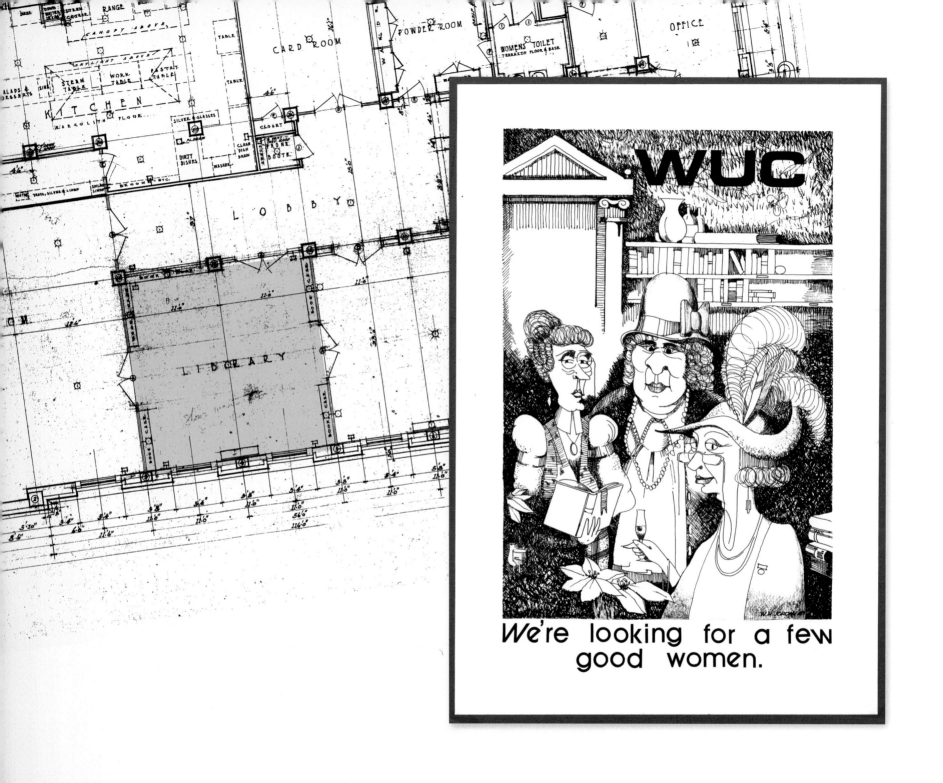

WUC

We're looking for a few good women.

Chapter 8

Modernizing ✣

OUR WONDERFUL YEAR WAS AN APPROPRIATE THEME FOR THE 1980 BIRTHDAY Party. Each member received a booklet entitled *Historical Highlights, 1914–1980*, an update of the Club's remarkable story that was specially prepared for the event by a small group selected by the History and Traditions Committee. During this sixty-sixth celebration of its founding, the Club honored sixty women who had been members for more than six decades, five of whom were charter members. (The last surviving charter member, Lottie Trenholme Hughes, passed away in 1985 at the age of ninety-four.)

Keeping members informed about events in the world at large and responding to their quest for new learning experiences were challenges the Club handled deftly. Literature classes offered in 1980 included favorites such as Book Review, Classical Literature, Philosophy, Poetry, and Creative Writing, as well as new trends in self-improvement such as Transactional Analysis. Standards of attire were more relaxed, with the hats and gloves of yesteryear long gone. Women in pants instead of skirts, and gentlemen in tieless shirts reflected the more casual look that was the norm during the day. In the evening, tradition still prevailed—men were to wear coats and ties, and ladies to wear dresses or nice pantsuits. The interests of members' young daughters took new directions, resulting in the end of the once-popular teen fashion shows.

Frugal management of Club facilities never went out of favor. It was evident in even the smallest of incidents. Longtime employee Judy Donnelly, who would become executive manager in 2003, recalled an anecdote about Charlotte Malone, then the secretary of the Club's board:

Bill Jordan, the multitalented husband of former president Wendy Jordan, created this humorous sketch of the ladies of the Club.

One day Mrs. Malone came into the accounting office to make some photocopies. . . . The glass doorknob fell off in her hand. She took a wooden match from her handbag, broke off a piece, shoved it together with the knob back into its original position and said in her sweet, raspy voice, "You know, I'm Scotch. I live in an old house and do this frequently. That will hold it for a while.

One noticeable shift in direction was a growing emphasis on privacy and exclusivity. From its inception the Club had welcomed publicity about its speakers, members, and activities, and the newspapers were eager to comply. When prominent speakers were scheduled, the Club heavily publicized them. They were made available to the media for interviews, and journalists were often in the audience. By the early eighties, however, press coverage had been steadily diminishing for more than a decade, making it more and more difficult to

Presidents ✣

Mary Bruce Lhamon	*1980–81*
Barbara McNicoll	*1981–82*
Ruth Soriano	*1982–83*
Mary Fran Hill	*1983–84*
Ellen Blom	*1984–85*
Nancy Layton	*1985–86*
Phyllis Mines	*1986–87*
Carol Jean Berg	*1987–88*
Cynthia Hamp	*1988–89*
Ruthie Kallander	*1989–90*

arrange publicity even for major speakers. The society page became the women's page and then disappeared altogether as "lifestyle" gained cachet. After reviewing the practices of other clubs, the board decided to discontinue pursuit of publicity for the Mainstream and Goodevening speakers.

Tolerance for smoking also decreased over the course of the decade. Cigarettes and cigars had been permitted throughout the Club for almost seventy years, but in 1984, months of discussion resulted in designated smoking and nonsmoking areas. The dining room provided a nonsmoking section and all classrooms were nonsmoking, with the exception of one room on each of the upper floors. This policy failed to satisfy either side in a debate growing rancorous not only in the clubhouse but around the country. The Club then tried posting signs—Thank You For Not Smoking—hoping that etiquette would triumph. It did not. By the end of the decade, the board had banned smoking throughout the Club except in the west end of the Gold Room.

The construction of the Crowne Plaza Hotel next door led to tense discussions in the early eighties. The hotel's manager met with board members and the Club manager to discuss the problems resulting from construction and the ongoing concerns about parking, waste disposal, and service deliveries. Not all issues were resolved; the line of taxis parked in front of the Club on Sixth Avenue waiting to pick up hotel guests finally prompted the board to write a letter to the Seattle City Council, which ordered the taxi rank moved to Seneca Street.

With the last mortgage payments in sight, board discussions focused on expanding the dining room onto the terrace. It was a proposal that did not enjoy widespread support, however. When the board hired an architect, a number of Club members petitioned for a special meeting at which the full membership voted against the project. Chastened, the board hired a consultant to analyze the way the existing space was used and design an attractive plan to redecorate the dining room—without expansion.

The dining room was not the only space that seemed inadequate for the Club's 1,600 members. Finding a space in which to schedule classes and programs was a constant struggle for trustees. In February 1982, the secretary recorded in the board minutes a droll account of one such problem:

> *[The Literature Trustee] expressed extreme displeasure that the first meeting of the new English Architecture and Stately Homes class was summarily moved from the ballroom to the Gold Room. Neither the trustee nor the class chairman was consulted. This was done to accommodate the Posting Party's sudden desire to give its program in the ballroom, rather than in the dining room where it has been held for at least 18 years. [The Trustee] sputtered a little when book discussion classes were moved out of the ballroom twice during the year; she was generous and understanding when Spring Arts Fair asked that there be no book review March 17 so that the ballroom could be set up for the Fair, but this time gentle readers she is LIVID. When events have been scheduled for the ballroom months in advance, have been on the club calendar for the same period of time, may the ballroom be rescheduled at will by whoever wishes it? She awaits an answer to the above question.*

Musicians and thespians, professional and amateur, continued to play starring roles in Club life. In 1983, conductor, pianist, and humorist George Shangrow began entertaining members with thrilling performances offered by a parade of musical talent during a series of classes originally titled "Enjoyment of Music." The Club's own Handbag Players presented a program, *Dash Through the Decades*, at the sixty-ninth Birthday Party; and a play scripted by member Norma Wills, *The Winner's Circle*, was a highlight of its seventieth. The same year, Drama Workshop was created to study theater performance and provide instruction in voice, diction, characterization, and improvisation. Over the years, many budding actresses were discovered and Club audiences were amused and delighted by the class members' variety of dramatic presentations, including the Frivolous Follies, a hugely successful vaudeville-style musical extravaganza that was so popular it was repeated several times in succeeding years.

During the 1980s, Mainstream and Goodevening were the Club's premier programs, each showcasing celebrated national speakers. Both were so well attended that an early reservation for the series' ticket subscriptions was essential. Single tickets would become available for sale only when a subscriber was unable to attend. The booklets of printed tickets for these events were so valued they were kept in the Club's safe until distributed.

Unfortunately, speaker fees rose dramatically in the 1980s, forcing the board to consider raising prices or reducing the number of programs. After much discussion, they responded with an initiative to create a special endowment or sustaining fund to underwrite major speakers. Just in time for the seventieth Birthday Party, the February 1984 *Bulletin* announced the initiative and encouraged members either to make a contribution to the Birthday Fund or to become inaugural donors to the new fund. President Mary Fran Hill said: "It is our hope to establish an endowment fund to help bring in more

outstanding programs. . . . Let us set the specific guidelines for its use—it is not set up for every event in trouble. It . . . is to be used to ensure the continuation of outstanding speakers as their costs escalate and our seating capacity remains constant."

Members rose to the challenge and contributed generously. The caliber of the programs supported by ticket purchases and the new Sustaining Fund remained extraordinary. Mainstream speakers included Nina S. Hyde, *Washington Post* fashion editor; Iris Love, author of *Love Among the Ruins;* Norman Cousins, chairman of the *Saturday Review* editorial board; dancer Cyd Charisse; and local personalities such as cartoonist David Horsey and Judge William Dwyer. Goodevening lectures featured Malcolm Forbes Jr.; Charles Osgood, CBS News commentator; Peter Duchin, composer and orchestra leader; Arthur Frommer, travel author and publisher; and David and Julie Eisenhower.

Left to right: President Cynthia Hamp; Carmel Quinn, star of radio, television, and Broadway; and member Patti Devin. Miss Quinn was featured at a Goodevening lecture in 1989.

As early as 1960, the board had investigated whether acquiring one of the new "computing machines" would be worth the expense. By the early 1980s, the time had clearly come. The 1983 purchase of a computer to handle billing may have been met at first with mistrust and consternation, but the new billing statements issued the following year showed a vast improvement. The Club acquired its first word processor in 1985 to use in preparing the *Bulletin*. Next came the computerization of the general ledger, followed by the financial reports, the accounting system, and the membership records, which were much easier to update when the U.S. Postal Service converted to the zip+4 code. The board soon realized the efficiency of having an all-inclusive database rather than individual systems. By 1987, their conquest of new technology qualified them as thoroughly modern Millies.

The WUCettes showing off their dance steps in April 1988

Let us entertain you!

FRIVOLOUS FOLLIES
8 PM ● APRIL 30
Presented by WUC Drama Workshop
Please make reservations early

The last Frivolous Follies was presented in 2002.

Gail Layman and Lee Wheeler perform an "Ole and Lena" routine at the Frivolous Follies, 2002

Although some moves into the digital era were made during these years, many board governance traditions practiced by the founders were still followed. The board was heavily involved in day-to-day minutiae, and financial decisions were frequently recorded in great detail in their meeting minutes: whether to buy a new copier, what kind, and the terms of the agreement with the copy company; what price to charge for rental of the Gold Room and how to inform the members of the change; whether to create a new ledger account for the costs of new-member orientation. The board had a strong hold on all details of Club management and expenditures, supervising every item bought or sold. By mid-decade, the Club manager was finally allowed to attend board meetings, but only to make specific reports.

One new, and somewhat short-lived, tradition did develop at board meetings—serving champagne to toast trustees' birthdays, perfect board attendance, the completion of the budget, and perhaps other noteworthy events not recorded. One secretary noted in the minutes: "Champagne arrived and we toasted [the treasurer] . . . and her budget, [the president] . . . for her terrific leadership, and all of us for having the foresight or whatever to see a good budget when it comes around. Cheers! Adjourned happily at 3 P.M."

In 1986, an important leadership change occurred with the retirement of Imogene Rogan, the Club's manager, from the "temporary" job she had occupied for twelve years. She was reinstated as a member and given a life membership in recognition of her many years of dedicated service. After a thoughtful search, Sheron Givan was hired to take her place.

Maintaining the Club's beautiful home was another top priority, but the requirements of the aging clubhouse were exceeding regular funding sources. In 1988, the board created a dedicated Capital Fund in memory of Margretta Hillman, president in 1940–41, who had died the previous year, to receive donations for the upkeep of the clubhouse. The Memorial and Gift Committee was assigned the task of oversight.

Dining room finances were also a concern despite a full, active membership. Expired dining credits, along with bar purchases, enabled the dining room to stay in the black most years. By the end of the decade, the board had increased the monthly dining minimum to $10 and loosened restrictions on which meals could be used against the credit.

In addition, entrance fees were raised from $400 to $650 for senior residents. A dues increase came in 1984 when the year showed a 27 percent increase in expenses. Parking rates in 1986 were $3.50 for three to five hours—if you could get in. An appraisal of all Club objets d'art stated their value at $169,855.

Club-sponsored outings were actively promoted and attended. Each summer the Club offered inviting opportunities for visits to locations far and near. In addition to the annual Ashland tour, summer ventures might include a garden tour by David Poot, one of Seattle's most respected landscape designers, or a bus trip to the Bloedel Reserve on Bainbridge Island. Members also toured Port Townsend's grand Victorian homes; took an overnight trip to Sun Mountain Lodge with stops in Winthrop and Leavenworth; picnicked at Quilcene during a performance of the Philadelphia String Quartet; and visited the famed Pilchuck Glass School in Stanwood.

Travel talks were almost as popular and enjoyable as traveling. In 1988, Edmonds native and travel writer Rick Steves spoke about his new book, *Europe Through the Back Door*, a publication full of tips and information for the enthusiastic budget traveler.

The domestic arts were enjoying their own success. The Cuisine class celebrated its fifteenth anniversary with birthday cake following lunch in the dining room. Guest chefs demonstrating their culinary artistry included Tom Douglas of Café Sport and Nancy Bishop of the Magnolia Cooking School. In addition, craft classes were multiplying in subject and number. Students during the 1988–89 season could choose from calligraphy, assembling Christmas decorations, stitchery, collage, basketmaking, and quilting. Fashion was always a crowd-pleasing attraction, and Club shows were a regular sellout.

George Shangrow was a dynamic force in the culture of the Women's University Club for over thirty years. His erudite lectures explored virtually every aspect of musical history and performance. "Friday at the Club with George" became a magnet for the Club's music lovers. In the mornings, besides sharing his vast knowledge in a way that was easy to understand, Mr. Shangrow brought scores of fellow musicians to entertain and delight his audience. In the afternoons he provided expert lecturers who prepared attendees for upcoming Seattle Opera performances.

Each December Mr. Shangrow presented a lovely bonus concert of holiday music sung by a quartet of local musicians that over the years included Carol (Kia) Sams, Jerry Sams, David Kechley, and Ann Erickson. At various times Mr. Shangrow and Mrs. Sams directed the WUC Chorus.

Mr. Shangrow was not easy to pin down. He always arranged entertaining and interesting programs, though they might not be exactly what had originally been planned. He never disappointed. He delighted in sharing his knowledge, and he was a font of storytelling and wisdom that never ceased to amaze. His lunch always began with a bowl of clam chowder, and his love of a good martini was legendary.

George Shangrow was ebullient, gregarious, unpredictable, and brimming with the joy of everything musical. Members of the Club were blessed to have known him and will forever treasure his memory.

George Shangrow is pictured here in 1988.

The Green Jays, a pair of porcelain birds by Edward Marshall Boehm (1913-1969), was given to the Club by Ruth Holland in about 1980. The artist is renowned for his porcelain depictions of natural subjects, and his birds are especially prized. Though Mrs. Holland was not a member of the Club, she always enjoyed visiting. She was the owner of the Pine Tree Tea Room, a popular spot in Seattle, and she often traded meals for pieces of work by local artists. Mrs. Holland owned many "Boehm birds." She donated most of the collection to the Frye Art Museum.

Over the years, the creation and display of posters for Club events was often a source of frustration and conflict. Committee chairmen, eager to attract attention to their events, kept making ever-larger posters. When the board finally regulated poster size and put the Publicity Trustee in charge of enforcement, peace in the multiyear "poster wars" seemed to have arrived. But the truce was only temporary. Conflict broke out again, this time centered on the placement and rotation of posters, as committee chairmen vied for the most visible location. A Poster Committee was established, which attempted at first to teach members how to make attractive posters that also met Club guidelines. It didn't work as well as planned, but it set the scene for a satisfying solution in 1989, under the Music, Arts and Crafts Trustee. The new Graphic Arts Committee, with cochairmen and a roster of artists, became the resource for designing and producing all posters made in the Club. Quality was assured through the use of more sophisticated techniques for lettering and illustrations. Guidelines eliminated all large posters in favor of permitting one 9 × 12-inch poster per event. Nine posters could be displayed on the framed bulletin board, and

space was available for eight more posters on an easel when needed. A committee simply had to submit a work order, and an artfully prepared poster would be ready for display before the event.

Change happens inexorably as the years turn into decades, and the eighties saw their share. At the beginning of the decade, smoking breaks occurred during classes; at the end, smoking had been banned almost everywhere—and would soon disappear altogether. For a large part of the decade, members still used titles such as "Mrs." and "Miss," and were as often identified by their husbands' given names as by their own, but by the end of the 1980s this formality had all but disappeared. The press's long love affair with the Club (and "society" news in general) came to an end, leaving the Publicity Trustee without a job. The trusteeship was combined with History and Traditions during 1981–83, then came under different trusteeships for several years, and finally was absorbed into Publications in 1989–90.

Even though the intrinsic value of the Club to its members could not be measured in dollars and cents, it was comforting to learn that the official assessed valuation was $3.24 million in 1988.

Members were ready to turn the page to a brand-new chapter.

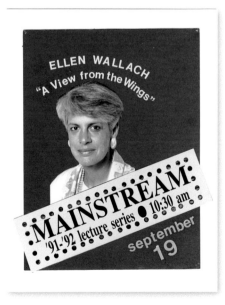

Several examples of posters created for various events at the Club in the late 1980s and early 1990s

Chapter 9

Planning Ahead ❧

OWARD THE END OF THE EIGHTIES, RECOGNIZING THAT PRIVATE CLUBS would inevitably be affected by the changing roles of women, work structures, and living patterns, the board embarked on a multiyear project to formulate a long-range strategic plan. The process engaged Club members and was designed to influence decisions throughout the nineties and beyond.

The board created a new Long-Range Planning Committee to "formulate and maintain a long-range plan by surveying, researching, analyzing, and addressing future challenges, opportunities, and potential for development of the Club." The committee surveyed members on a variety of topics and established five groups: Communications, to study how the Club communicated with members; Administration, Governance and Budget, to examine board, staff, and steering committee structures; Services, to look at travel and tours, classes, and programs; Clubhouse, to research capital requirements for maintenance and historic preservation status; and Personnel, to consider recommendations for employees' pay and benefits.

During the next several years, the Long-Range Planning Committee analyzed every aspect of Club operations, with the goal of learning how best to use its resources to assure a flourishing future. They considered a wide range of possibilities: admitting men to full membership, which they recommended against; giving awards to outstanding women in the community, which came to fruition as the Brava! Award program in 2003; forming a Real Estate Asset Management Committee and merging the Building and Decorating Committees into one entity, both of which became a reality.

Watercolor of the clubhouse by WUC painting instructor Julie Creighton

The board also completed some "housekeeping" duties to help make club operations run more smoothly. They revised and updated the Club policy guide, known as the *Policies, Procedures, and Responsibilities Handbook* (PPR), and standardized contracts for speakers, teachers, performers, and others who were paid to appear at Club functions. Chairmen were asked, if possible, not to schedule classes on the days of major Club functions, which the board defined in 1991 as all Traditional Events, important lectures, the fall or spring fashion show, and the Spring Arts Fair. No meals were to be served outside of the dining room during these events.

At the May 1991 Annual Meeting, both outgoing president Carol Batchelder and incoming president Joyce McCallum spoke about the changed realities of private clubs. They emphasized that continuing education distinguished the Women's University Club from other clubs in the city and that the organization was in a strong financial position with a beautiful clubhouse. But there were significant challenges as well: decreasing membership, rising costs, inadequate parking,

Presidents ❧

President	Years
Carol Batchelder	1990–91
Joyce McCallum	1991–92
Bonita Dennison	1992–93
Wendy Jordan	1993–94
Gail Layman	1994–95
Marcia Peterson	1995–96
Darlene Jones	1996–97
Gail Coie	1997–98
Carol Gaffner	1998–99
Kathy Judkins	1999–00

and increasing traffic on the city's streets and highways, which was making access to the Club difficult at times.

At the November 1991 Semiannual Meeting, President McCallum remarked on what might indeed be regarded as the Club's secret ingredient, in spite of its challenges—the energy of its members. She reported that there were 65 different classes and events on the fall schedule, and 1,105 members were either chairing or serving on committees.

Over the next several years, members continued to experiment with fresh ideas for classes and recruit interesting speakers. A new literature class, titled Learning about Women: From Beowulf to Colonial Times, made its debut in 1992. The Mainstream series continued its success, supported in part by generous gifts to the Memorial Endowment Fund. Jill Ker Conway, popular author of the best-selling memoir *The Road from Coorain*, was one of its acclaimed speakers in 1992.

The next year, another innovative class, First Nighters, offered previews of plays at local theaters—similar to the opera previews members had enjoyed for many years. In 1990, the Goodevening series changed its name to Best of the Northwest, but its lineup of excellent speakers continued, although with a distinctly Northwest flavor. The 1993 schedule included Dr. Leroy Hood on modern genetic engineering, Judge William Dwyer on the legal aspects of trial by jury, and

true-crime writer Ann Rule on conducting research for her books. That summer, the Ashland trip was enhanced with a side trip to the Oregon Coast and a backstage tour of one of the Oregon Shakespeare Festival theaters. Two busloads of Club members made the pilgrimage.

Another experiment significantly improved the way Club news was disseminated. Communication with members had always been a priority. Starting in 1914, a printed monthly notice of all activities—from speakers, to classes in shoemaking, to bylaws revisions and calls for help rolling Red Cross bandages—was mailed to members. A simple pamphlet at first, it gradually changed size, colors, and appearance, becoming known as the *Bulletin*. For seventy-five years, this small publication carried all the Club news. But the amount of information was exceeding its capacity. In 1989, President Ruthie Kallander inaugurated a four-page *President's Letter* to supplement the *Bulletin*.

Because the *Letter* provided so much more editorial flexibility, it was a natural prelude to the creation of a monthly, multipage newsletter that would completely replace the now-inadequate little *Bulletin*. President Bonita Dennison and the board approved the concept at their summer retreat, and in September 1992 the first edition of *WUC News* was published. Advances in technology—state-of-the-art computers and sophisticated copying equipment—made it possible to progress from simple black-and-white to full color on quality paper stock and eventually to print, staple, and fold 1,200 copies in the clubhouse.

Not all traditions made sense as the Club evaluated its operations. Name Clearing, which started in the 1920s, was an annual ritual in which trustees laid claim to the women they wanted to serve as committee chairmen. It had arisen because a set of rules dating back decades defined who could chair a committee, prohibited members from chairing more than one committee, and limited the number of committees on which a member could serve.

Each year, usually in April, the trustees engaged in a bidding war for committee chairmen governed by elaborate guidelines that occupied pages in the board policy manual. Duplicate requests for the same chairman were settled through bargaining and negotiation among the trustees. The ongoing evaluation of Club procedures targeted this complicated, unwieldy tradition early on, and the board quickly abandoned it without a backward glance.

The strategic planning process continued to generate recommendations for other improvements. In 1993, the trusteeships were reorganized. Changes included moving Creative Writing from the Programs Trustee to Communication Arts and consolidating all of the speakers' programs under the Programs Trustee. In another break with tradition, the Club's executive manager, Sheron Givan, was invited to address the members at the 1994 Annual Meeting. Mrs. Givan spoke about the educational attainments of key staff members, all of whom were engaged in some form of continuing education to receive the highest credential in their respective fields.

At the same Annual Meeting, mindful of the many initiatives still in the planning stages, incoming president Wendy Jordan reminded members of a Michigan football coach's recipe for success: "a wishbone to dream with and shape our vision . . . a backbone for strength and courage to fulfill our dreams . . . and a funny bone to laugh at silly things that go amiss." At the end of her term, following a series of discussions about the Club's investment policy, the board approved the creation of a five-member Investment Committee appointed by the president and chaired by the treasurer. The Corporate Finance and Operating Finance Committees were consolidated at the same time.

Without a doubt, 1995 and 1996 were years of significant change at the Club. Members approved creating a president-elect position and simplifying membership categories, granting associate members full privileges, and combining a number of committees. The board was also authorized to increase dues and fees as often as once a year without a vote of the membership. In a reversal of the Club's practice since its inception, the executive manager became a regular participant in board meetings. The revolution in management practices was reflected in the 1996 board's motto: "Respect for tradition and enthusiasm for innovation."

Throughout these years, members demonstrated their continuing affection for the Club with a steady stream of gifts, large and small,

The new Steinway was presented to the Club at the Piano Gala in November 1990. Featured artist was Daniel Pollack.

Shirley Fleischmann, Daniel Pollack and President Carol Batchelder at the Piano Gala

Left to right: Doris Totten Chase, painter, sculptor, and video artist; with Ardelle Ennis and Ellie Russell

The Club has produced a monthly publication since its founding. Small bulletins were replaced by newsletters beginning in 1989. Changes in the Club logo are evident over the years.

for various capital and operating projects. In 1990, a bequest from the estate of Charlotte Malone allowed the Spring Room to be redecorated; it was renamed the Malone Room in her memory.

In 1994, the Opal Orr Fund was established with a bequest, to be used as "a memorial endowment for educational lectures and programs which benefit all." Actress Claire Bloom was the first speaker sponsored by the new fund. With the increase in this form of giving, the Edith Backus Society was created in 1998 to recognize members who included the Club in their estate planning.

While the Long-Range Planning Committee was occupied with fundamental questions about the Club's future, members were actively shaping day-to-day connections. One of the initiatives was a renewal of the community involvement that had been a hallmark of the war years. In 1996, the board began choosing one or two charities as holiday service projects. In addition, members began organizing opportunities, carried out under the auspices of the Club, to volunteer on behalf of a variety of nonprofit organizations.

Nowhere was the influence of members more evident than in the dining room. When the board, in spite of increasing demand, could not justify paying for a commercial espresso machine, a member with a passion for coffee donated one. When spouses began asking about serving draft beer, another member provided the gift of a keg cooler. At the first Summer Crab Feed in 1991, 150 people consumed all 210 pounds of crab that had been purchased. The event was so well received that it became a regular part of the summer program. Later in the decade, the menu moved away from comfort food designed with older members in mind, such as meat loaf or liver and onions, to selections more in tune with younger members, such as the "bistro" fare in the Gold Room, where "casual Friday" attire was acceptable. Later changes included serving complimentary afternoon tea and cookies in the Drawing Room and offering private-label wines.

Underlying all of the strategic considerations was the fundamental question: What kind of physical identity should the Club have? Should it add athletic facilities, or return to operating hotel-like guest facilities? Should it tear down the garage and dining room and build an addition on that footprint, or sell the existing building and land,

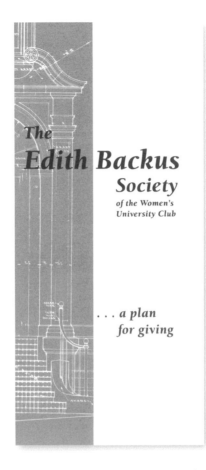

The Edith Backus Society was created in 1998. This fund encourages members to remember the Club in their estate plans with a deferred bequest of $5,000 or more. Gifts are used for the benefit of future generations of members.

and buy property nearby? In 1990, the Club briefly considered purchasing the adjacent Kennedy Hotel (now the Hotel Vintage Park) but decided against it. The same year, President Carol Batchelder met with representatives of a developer to discuss the possibility of putting a high-rise building of forty to forty-five stories on the Club's property, either through a ground lease or in partnership. It would take more than two years to complete construction, and the question was—what would happen to the Club's members and the activities in which they participated in the meantime?

The conversation continued internally, with members deeply divided on the subject. In October 1997, ten board members and President Gail

The Garden, an oil painting by Leonard Wren, was purchased in 1997 with donations from members of the Club. Mr. Wren is considered one of the most important American impressionist artists of the twentieth century.

Coie visited seven private clubs in Philadelphia, including two women's clubs, to investigate how they were dealing with the challenges of operating city clubs. They returned convinced that the Club's wisest course of action was to preserve its heritage on Sixth Avenue and Spring Street with ongoing modernization and upgrades to the clubhouse, while undertaking new approaches to membership growth. In an open letter to members, published in the *WUC News* after their return, the president wrote: "We felt very proud of our Club as we compared it to the ones we saw. Our clubhouse is very special, our members are interesting and stimulating, and our program of classes, events and lectures was the envy of everyone we met."

Parking had driven much of the real estate discussions during the nineties and remained an issue once the decision to stay in place was made. One of the earliest attempts to add parking capacity involved the nearby Crowne Plaza Hotel. While the effort never bore fruit, it did generate an amusing anecdote, as President Gail Layman (1994–95) recalled:

> We . . . had many meetings with the Crowne Plaza Hotel next door about a cooperative effort to increase space for both [of] us. . . . This never materialized but it was an exciting process. I remember we were going to tell the membership about the discussions at the Semi-Annual Meeting. I went to Book Review that morning and told the audience that I hoped they would come to the meeting because I had an exciting announcement. A friend in the audience said later that she heard one older member lean over to another member and say, "Oh, how exciting! I bet she is going to tell us she is pregnant." Oh, my, I was one of the younger presidents at that time, but not that young. I have never forgotten the compliment. It still makes me smile.

Other attempts to lease parking spaces or make reciprocal arrangements with nearby lots were unsuccessful. In 1999, after a decade-long search for solutions, the possibility of a valet parking system was raised. It was unanimously accepted, and with the hiring of a valet service, the Club's parking problems were solved—at least for a time.

lint Prescott became executive manager in February 1998. After his arrival, the board took an important step in the modernization process, giving up its responsibility for day-to-day decisions and turning personnel and other matters over to the executive manager. He outlined a technology upgrade plan that included establishing a computer network at the Club, moving to Microsoft Windows 98 and compatible programs, and evaluating the accounting system. Within a few weeks, the Club had its first e-mail account for limited use by staff and trustees.

During the nineties, corrections and improvements to governance and business operations simplified and reinvigorated Club life for members—and paved the way for future possibilities. With the Long-Range Planning Committee steering the course, a professional manager in the driver's seat, and valet parking, the Club headed into 2000 at a good clip on a smooth road.

LOOK WHO'S SUPPORTING THE **WUC**

1991-1992 BUILDING COMMITTEE

Another of Bill Jordan's drawings, this one of the clubhouse

During summer closure in 1993, the silk wall covering in the dining room was removed in preparation for redecoration.

HOME   ABOUT US   JOIN   PRIVATE EVENTS   GUEST INFORMATION   CONTACT US   MEMBERS' AREA

WUC

WOMEN'S UNIVERSITY CLUB
OF SEATTLE

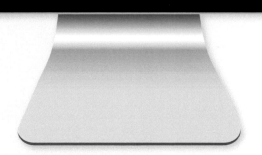

Home | About Us | Join | Private Events | Guest Information | Contact Us | Members' Area

Beginning a New Century ❧

F THE NINETIES WAS A DECADE IN WHICH THE CLUB REEXAMINED ALL of its internal workings, the first decade of the twenty-first century was one in which the Club turned outward and began to reengage with the broader community. It was a big step for a Club that had grown to cherish its privacy, but one that brought it closer to the outlook of its earliest members. After all, marketing had begun under a Publicity Trustee—in 1919.

To give focus to outreach efforts, the Board of Trustees developed a new Marketing Trusteeship in 1999. The title of the position changed five times between then and 2013—from "Marketing" to "Community Relations" to "Marketing and Community Connections"—but its purpose remained to "develop and implement new strategies to make the presence of the Club known in the community and to support and/or publicize nonprofit volunteer opportunities." The Club's priorities for community involvement were programs benefiting education, women, and children.

Outreach came gradually and with little fanfare. As early as 1997, Club members were answering phones for the local public television station telethon, as well as gathering pledges for long-distance walks benefiting heart disease research. That involvement expanded in the new century to include YWCA projects and programs, helping at the FareStart restaurant, giving to First Place School, and sponsoring Cancer Survivors' Luncheons, among other projects. When Hurricane Katrina devastated New Orleans in August 2005, the Club organized a campaign to contribute to hurricane relief through the Red Cross in collaboration with U.S. Bank's matching gift program. It was the first time since World War II that the Club had mounted such a fund-raising drive.

In many ways, the various plans adopted by the board in the years following the turn of the new century were more reminiscent of the Club of the forties than the Club of the eighties. Aiming to be "Puget Sound's preeminent women's club located in downtown Seattle," the board defined the Club's values as lifelong learning and personal growth, governance by members, community involvement, and service. The latter two had been lost in the turmoil of the sixties and seventies, then forgotten in the complacency of the eighties, but were now restored as an essential part of the Club's mission.

Presidents ❧

Lailla Petersen	2000–01	Suzanne Price	2007–08
Janis Johnson	2001–02	Ann Linnell	2008–09
Corinne Hill	2002–03	Rosalie King	2009–10
Judith Harper	2003–04	Bonnie Miller	2010–11
Karen Smith	2004–05	Donna Walzer	2011–12
Linda Beecher	2005–06	Mary Kraft	2012–13
Joy Goodenough	2006–07	Suzy Lantz	2013–14

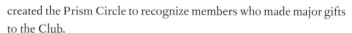
November 7, 2000	George W. Bush is elected president
January 1, 2001	University of Washington Huskies play their 14th Rose Bowl game
February 28, 2001	Nisqually earthquake measures 6.8 on the Richter scale
September 11, 2001	World Trade Center towers collapse, Pentagon is severely damaged, and a passenger plane crashes in terrorist attacks
October 7, 2001	U.S. launches invasion of Afghanistan
July 20, 2002	New Seahawks stadium opens
March 19, 2003	U.S. invasion of Iraq begins
May 23, 2004	New Seattle Central Library opens
January 20, 2007	Seattle Art Museum's Olympic Sculpture Park opens
November 4, 2008	Barack Obama is elected as first African American president
September 16, 2010	Seattle Storm wins second WNBA national championship (first was in 2004)

During the Nisqually earthquake on February 28, 2001, which measured 6.8 on the Richter scale, staff evacuated 120 people from the Club's building in less than five minutes. The quake caused extensive damage to masonry buildings in Pioneer Square, but the exterior of the little clubhouse on the hill was relatively unscathed. Measuring devices were installed to monitor interior wall surface cracking, and a report on earthquake damage concluded that the building was structurally sound. Nevertheless, there wasn't a room in which the lath-and-plaster walls hadn't suffered, and a great deal of repair work was required. Summer closure that year lasted the entire month of July to accommodate the necessary plastering, painting, masonry work, and wallpapering.

Gifts continued to add an extra dimension to the Club experience. In 2002, the Memorial and Gift Committee

Member Dorothie Knoblauch was an inveterate traveler. "I'm very, very curious," she said. "If I hear anything I don't know about, if anything comes up in anything I read, I look it up right away." She often lectured on architecture at the Club.

created the Prism Circle to recognize members who made major gifts to the Club.

A bequest from Dorothie Knoblauch funded the installation of a new sound system in the Ballroom and brought a regular program of local professional theater to the Club.

A beautiful porcelain punch bowl was given by a gentleman who had no connection to the Club other than having enjoyed being a guest, but who wanted to give a "good home" to the circa 1770 museum-quality family treasure made in England.

In 2010, when the Memorial and Gift Committee established a Centennial Society Fund to honor the Club's 100th anniversary and support activities during the centennial year, the $100,000 goal was fully subscribed in three months.

In October 2002, with renewed enthusiasm for engagement with the broader community, the board created a committee to develop an idea that had first been mentioned by the Long-Range Planning Committee in the early nineties—establishing an award to recognize women who have made outstanding contributions to the community. Originally conceived as the Women's University Club Women of Excellence Award, it quickly became known as the Brava! Award. In the first year, members nominated forty-eight women. The first recipients were Virginia Anderson, director of Seattle Center; Francia Russell, co-artistic director of Pacific Northwest Ballet; and Rita Ryder, director of the YWCA of Seattle, King County and Snohomish County.

As planning for the first awards ceremony went forward, the Marketing Trustee suggested raising money from members for a scholarship to be presented, in connection with the Brava! Awards, to an outstanding young woman graduating from a local high school. Letters sent to guidance counselors produced forty scholarship nominations that year. The first event, held on June 1, 2003, was such a success that the scholarship fund and the Brava! Awards remained an important part of the Club year more than a decade later.

The scholarship fund became a 501(c)(3) charitable organization in 2004. Over the years, the number of scholarships awarded annually to high school graduates increased from one to three. In 2008, with administrative assistance from the YWCA, a fourth scholarship was added for a woman in transition. This award was typically given to a woman returning to school to improve her life circumstances.

Adapting to changes in technology became a way of life in the new century. One of the first steps taken was the development of a website that went online in September 2000. Within months, the dining room began accepting e-mail reservations, and the e-mail addresses of members were soon included in the Directory. A computer installed in the Kachina Annex permitted members to work online directly from the Club. The website evolved as the Club explored the many ways it could be used to serve members and inform the public, with substantial upgrades in 2005 and a major redesign in 2009.

Constant fine-tuning of the organization had also become ingrained in the Club's practices. In a 2001 bylaws change, members delegated determination of the maximum number of members to the board. Perhaps in a nod to sensitive feelings, senior members became known as resident members. Management of parking became an executive manager responsibility in 2004. The next year, the board changed the fiscal year from May 1–April 30 to September 1–August 31 to better reflect the actual program year.

A significant change occurred in June 2003, when executive manager Clint Prescott resigned. The assistant manager, Judy Donnelly, who had started at the Club as a receptionist in 1980, accepted the position of executive manager. Because she had held many positions in the Club over the previous twenty-three years— chief accountant, publications supervisor, and food and beverage manager—Judy understood Club operations from the ground up. Chef Tino Laciste was hired the same month. In August, the new chef introduced the Beers, Burgers and Berries Bash, which quickly became a summer mainstay.

Innovation in programs and classes paralleled innovation in operations. With Best of the Northwest, Mainstream, and the Carrie B. Raser Fund all arranging for outstanding speakers, there was always a worthwhile program to attend. European travel guru Rick Steves, Seattle Art Museum director Mimi Gardner Gates, and Bellevue Art Museum director Diane Douglas were among a long list of

Members working as waitstaff at FareStart, a popular Community Connections activity, are pictured here in 2012.

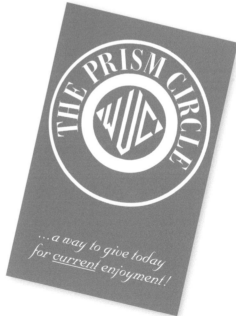

Prism Circle members are those who contribute $2,500 or more to fulfill current Club needs in ways that benefit the entire membership.

Brava!

The 2002–03 Board of Trustees established the Brava! Award to honor women who have provided positive, enduring contributions to the community. Nominations are received from Club members and outside organizations. Winners have included women in the arts, education, science, public service, sports, business, law, and technology. These women have started schools for the disadvantaged, flown in space, won the Nobel Prize, produced films, founded theaters, written books, published newspapers, started nonprofits, and put Seattle on the cutting edge of fashion design. The achievements and actions of the winners have removed barriers to success and opened up opportunities for other women. Each spring, the Club hosts a gala event to honor its Brava! Award winners and Women's University Club Foundation scholarship recipients. The award is the Club's way of saying thank you to the many women in the Seattle area who make our community a better place to live and who serve as positive role models for future generations of women.

Brava! Awards are presented each year to women who have made a lasting difference in their community. Pictured here are award winners and scholarship recipients in 2010.

prominent local figures who spoke at the Club early in the decade. National Public Radio personalities Susan Stamberg, Ray Suarez, and Rob Gifford appeared at the lectern, as did authors Jonathan Raban and Gail Sheehy.

Working members drove a number of changes in programs. One of the most significant was the addition of the CEO Executive Forum Luncheon in 2002–03.

Speakers such as William S. Ayer, president and CEO of Alaska Airlines; Alan Mulally, president and CEO of Boeing Commercial Airplanes; Jeff Brotman, cofounder and chairman of Costco; Blake Nordstrom, president of Nordstrom; and Mark Pigott, CEO of Paccar, offered members a window on the business world that had seldom been available before.

In 2004, the Programs Trustee proposed that Best of the Northwest and Mainstream be merged into a single speakers' series, offering both local and national speakers at either lunch or dinner. The new program became known as ViewPoint.

The same year, the Education Committee asked the Programs Trustee to organize a Children's Programs Committee.

Among their first offerings were a manners class and the appearance of Alexandra Day, author of *Good Dog, Carl*, a huge hit with parents and children alike. Summer movie evenings, a revival of the Halloween Party, a Christmas craft workshop, a teddy bear picnic, and many other programs followed. In the dining room, the annual Santa Brunch was augmented with evening Lego and train parties with the children of members in mind.

Women's University Club staff members and their years of service
Back row (left to right): Ronnie Caluza (9), Kevin Fisher (1), Jessie Rivera (35), Jesus Martinez (10), Luke Fosler (5), Judy Donnelly (34), Michael Koenig (15), Shannan Genest (13), Jacobo Martinez-Garcia (9)
Front row (left to right): Tino Laciste (10), Allen Rice (21), Estele Rualo (20), Mina Khastou (3), Kimberly Martin (5), Jaimie Sharpe (4), Sue Frederick (10), Fandy Lee (13), Jessica Vasquez (12)

In 2006, the first In the Spotlight Breakfast was held. It gave members an opportunity to speak about their careers and other interests, from starting a company to collecting Southeast Asian textiles. In 2009, the program was moved to Wednesday evenings to coincide with the popular hors d'oeuvres service. A year later, the Business and Professional Women's Group began holding regular meetings at the same time. Soon outside speakers such as business consultant Jan McLaughlin added thought-provoking perspectives to the mix.

Those interested in the Club's more traditional offerings were busy as well. A new Book Discussion class led by Sandy Eaker was added in 2002, and other book groups formed at lunch and in the evening. As its 100th anniversary approached, the Club had four separate book clubs meeting at diverse hours of the day and evening, and the revered Book Review class, with its weekly lectures on new books, was still going strong. The Literature Trustee's report to the board in March 2009 spoke eloquently to the wide range of offerings: the film *The Lives of Others* was shown; the Book Discussion class talked about Margaret Atwood's *Alias Grace;* Poetry discussed Nikki Giovanni's work; Religion offered a lecture on "Monasticism East and West"; and Classic and Modern Literature heard a lecture on seventeenth-century English poet George Herbert.

Seattle Opera's Perry Lorenzo, who had often spoken at the Club, began a lecture series in 2005–06 focusing on literary masterworks by Dante, Shakespeare, and Goethe. Each year until his death in 2009, Mr. Lorenzo brought his distinct perspective to topics throughout the Western canon of literature, art, and music; his series was one of the Club's most popular programs. Art historian Rebecca Albiani also had a large following at the Club during the earlier years of the new century. She gave a lecture in 2004 on "Kindred Spirits"—the partnerships of artists Georgia O'Keeffe and Alfred Stieglitz, Frida Kahlo and Diego Rivera, and Lee Krasner and Jackson Pollock—and went on to develop a popular lecture series focused on art.

After many years in which the Club sponsored only a few day trips, more extensive travel resumed in 2010 with a trip to Cambridge University in England, where members attended a two-week session of the International Summer School. Two years later, members spent a week at the Shakespeare Festival in Ashland, Oregon, with the trip preceded by lectures on the Shakespeare plays they would see.

Smaller changes included the introduction of an informal monthly luncheon group of women who enjoyed wearing hats and of an international luncheon, held every summer, at which students in the Club's language classes reunited for a menu of French, Spanish, and Italian fare. The Twelfth Night celebration returned in 2009 after an absence of many years. The one casualty of the early twenty-first century was the Frivolous Follies, which made its last appearance in 2002.

A few of the logos used to advertise
the Club's many programs

In 2007, the Club was approached about listing the clubhouse on the city register of historic places. Early the following year, several board members met with the Seattle Landmarks Preservation Board. The members expressed concern about listing the 1962 dining room addition and the garage underneath—the addition was not historic, and the Club wished to preserve the option of replacing it with something else or adding a structure on top of it. Further, a tour of the building suggested that nothing on the inside was truly historic, except perhaps the fireplace. With those reservations, the board fully supported listing the original 1922 building.

The Landmarks Preservation Board later voted unanimously to nominate the exterior of the 1922 building, excluding the interior and dining room addition. The Trustees also applied for, and received, national designation as a site of historic significance. In May 2010, Historic Seattle honored the Women's University Club for Exemplary Stewardship at its second annual awards ceremony, held at the Club.

A busy schedule of interior work continued. Gifts made at the Club's ninety-third Birthday Party permitted the refurbishment of the Lyle Room in traditional Federalist style—considered especially appropriate because of Mrs. Lyle's long involvement with the Mount Vernon Ladies' Association.

In 2008, the Long-Range Planning Committee recommended transforming the existing Scholarship Foundation into the Women's University Club Foundation.

WUC

WOMEN'S UNIVERSITY CLUB
FOUNDATION

One of the most popular events sponsored by the Children and Family Committee is the annual Halloween Party.

Perry Lorenzo, of Seattle Opera's Education Department, was one of the Club's most popular lecturers. His introduction to the Club began as a speaker at Best of the Northwest in 1996. In 2002, he became a regular lecturer at the Religions of the World series, in which he taught "Perspectives on the Arts and Religions with an Emphasis on Music." His annual series included "Religion in Literature," "Three Classic Poets: Dante, Shakespeare, Goethe," "Athens in the Fifth Century B.C.," and his final program, "In the Midst of the Middle Ages."

Mr. Lorenzo was a teacher by profession. His lectures were carefully prepared, delivered with clarity, amply illustrated by visuals or music, and exactly filled the hour and a half allotted. He rewarded capacity audiences with his broad knowledge, insights, humor, and glorious illustrations.

As a person, Mr. Lorenzo was warm, approachable, and eager to answer questions and share his passion for music, art, films, literature, and Catholicism. He died of cancer in 2009. The Club was enriched by the gifts of this genuine Renaissance man.

The committee proposed that historic preservation be added to the purposes for which the foundation might receive and dispense funds. In March 2009, after lengthy discussion, President Ann Linnell proposed a Women's University Club Foundation with three objectives, each governed by a council of three: scholarships, historic preservation of the building's exterior, and education. The board established the foundation the following month, and in May the newly appointed foundation board elected former Club president Lailla Petersen as its first chairman. In addition to continuing its scholarship awards, the foundation launched a campaign to restore the historic windows of the clubhouse and reached beyond the clubhouse walls with its Music Counts! program to support music education in public schools.

As the Club's 100th anniversary neared, the combination of tradition and innovation, the very heart of the Club's success, had become a way of life. While the Club's vision remained much the same as ever, it was expressed in new words: "The Women's University Club is the premier club in Seattle for dynamic, educated women." The Club could celebrate having fully lived the thoughtful goals of its members for 100 years: exceed expectations, celebrate success, and stay relevant.

The Club was recognized by the Governor's Advisory Council on Historic Preservation. The clubhouse is on the city, state, and national registers of historic places.

The porcelain punch bowl displayed in the dining room was made by the Plymouth Porcelain Company of Plymouth, England, circa 1770. The bowl features hand-painted flowers on the interior and exterior, and a free-form cobalt-blue design laced in gold vines and stylized leaves. It was given to the Club by the Abercrombie family, and is thought to have been among the family's possessions for 250 years. Though the family was not directly connected to the Club, they felt that it would be the perfect home for their precious antique.

This celadon bowl was purchased by the Decorating Committee, at the request of the Memorial and Gift Committee, from a bequest in memory of Arline Betts.

Starry Night on Sixth and Spring
watercolor by Charlette Haugen

Reflections

This history of the Women's University Club is full of remarkable stories. Those interested in world affairs debated the League of Nations in 1920 and studied the Arab Spring in 2012. Those who enjoyed needle arts embroidered napkins for the new clubhouse in 1922 and learned to sew with Ultrasuede in the 1970s. And, always, they read: Edna Ferber and Willa Cather in the early years, Hilary Mantel and Ian McEwan as their centennial drew near.

They were pragmatic, resourceful, and fearless leaders. The Club threw open its doors to Red Cross auxiliaries during World War I, sold more than $500,000 worth of war bonds during World War II, seized the opportunity to acquire property in anticipation of the need for expansion, and stayed downtown when the trickle of people and businesses to the suburbs became a flood. Members discussed, debated, and often disagreed, but their common vision always carried them through.

Although members have not shared the same economic status, political views, or life experiences, they have all brought energy, curiosity, and a commitment to lifelong learning to the Women's University Club. They have gained lasting friendships and the deep satisfaction of sharing simple pleasures with women they respect and admire. Here is how some of them have described it:

"The Women's University Club offers me the opportunity to meet, connect, and learn from amazing, energetic, and inspirational women. I believe this makes me a better individual."

"Every member is accepted and honored for who she is. . . . A member . . . is defined by her interests, her enthusiasms, her willingness to be part of the conversation. And conversations abound at the WUC!"

"Here is civility at its best; here is a wonderfully fertile place for forming deep, meaningful friendships."

"To me the WUC is three things: great women, great programs/classes, and a lovely, elegant place to relax, learn, or work. . . . I have never been with a group that is more supportive and kind."

"The Women's University Club is a priceless jewel, and we shall continue to cherish and protect it, for we cannot replace it, nor find what it offers anywhere else."

It is not only members who have remarked on the rare experience that is the Women's University Club. After visiting an Autumn Breakfast, Virginia Boren reported in her *Seattle Times* column of September 18, 1941:

Yesterday I saw . . . women of versatility, women of achievement, women of broad vision, women of eager minds, women alert to the present international situation, women who never settle back comfortably into snugly upholstered ruts, women who keep pace with progress. . . .

The greatest testament to the Club's founders is the way their grand idea has been cherished by the generations that have succeeded them. As longtime member Virginia Dearborn reflected in an essay written in 1992, "Whatever the future brings, we shall always build, as the past has done, upon the foresight of our beloved Founding Mothers, upon the firm foundation they provided us."

The drawing room at the Women's University Club

Notes & Credits

Notes

In the early years of the Club, women often referred to themselves by their married names ("Mrs. Alvah L. Carr"). In deference to the practice of the times, and to assist future historians, we have included husbands' names in parentheses through the 1940s.

The 1922 blueprints of the clubhouse prepared by Edouard Champney and Abraham Albertson have been used as illustrations throughout this volume.

Credits